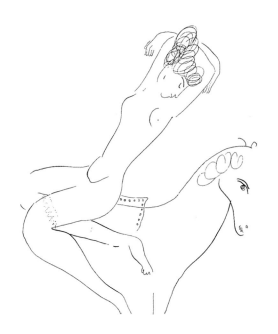

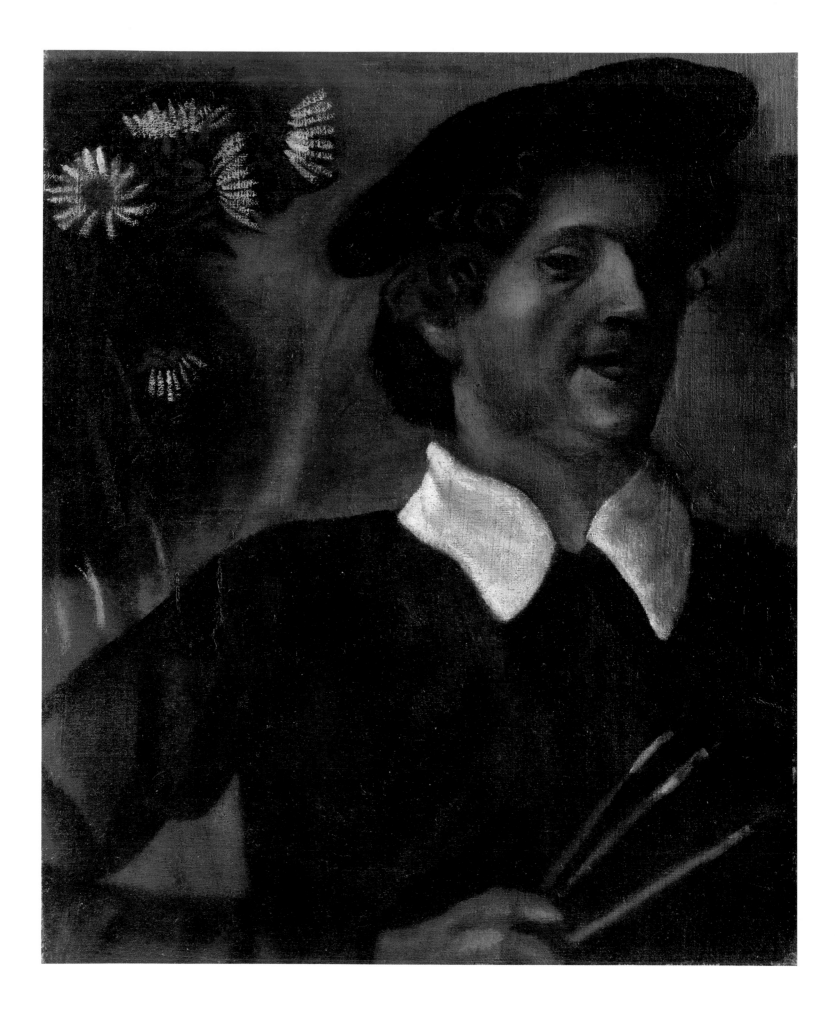

Ingo F. Walther/Rainer Metzger

Marc Chagall

1887–1985

Painting as Poetry

TASCHEN

To stay informed about upcoming TASCHEN titles,
please request our magazine at www.taschen.com/magazine or write to
TASCHEN America, 6671 Sunset Boulevard, Los Angeles, CA 90028, USA;
contact-us@taschen.com; Fax: +1-323-463-4442.
We will be happy to send you a free copy of our magazine,
which is filled with information about all of our books.

© 2012 TASCHEN GmbH
Hohenzollernring 53, D-50672 Köln
www.taschen.com

Original edition: © 2006 TASCHEN GmbH
© for the illustrations: VG Bild-Kunst, Bonn 2012
General editor: Ingo F. Walther, Alling
English translation: Michael Hulse, Cologne
Cover design: Sense/Net Art Direction, Andy Disl and
Birgit Eichwede, Cologne, www.sense-net.net
Final artwork: Tanja da Silva, Cologne

Printed in China
ISBN 978–3–8365–3114–6

Contents

6
Russia: The Early Years
1887–1910

14
The Paris Years
1910–1914

34
War and Revolution in Russia
1914–1923

50
France and America
1923–1948

76
The Late Work
1948–1985

92
Marc Chagall 1887–1985
A Chronology

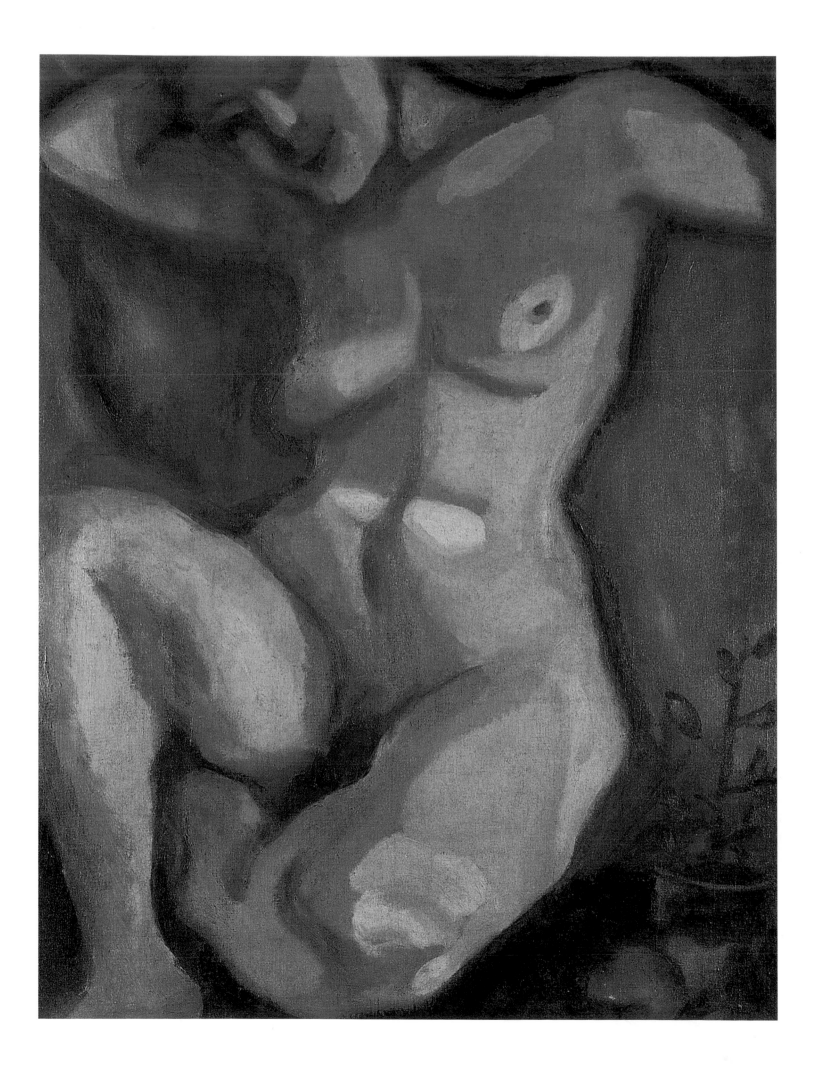

Russia: The Early Years
1887–1910

Marc Chagall: poet, dreamer, exotic apparition. Throughout his long life, the role of outsider and artistic eccentric came naturally to him. Chagall seemed a kind of intermediary between worlds: whether as a Jew with a lordly disdain for the ancient ban on image-making, or as a Russian who ventured beyond the realm of familiar self-sufficiency, or as the son of poor parents, growing up in a large and needy family, yet going on to establish himself in the sophisticated world of elegant artistic salons. The potential for assimilation and the liberality that distinguish Western culture are best assessed by its responses to outsiders; and Chagall personified the singular charm of the outsider his whole life long. His biography was far from everyday, and its reflection in his art took on the form of strange images. His life and art together added up to this image of a lonesome visionary, a citizen of the world with much of the child still in him, a stranger lost in wonder – an image that the artist did everything to cultivate. Profoundly religious and with a deep love of the homeland, his work is arguably the most urgent appeal for tolerance and respect of all that is different that modern times could make.

Marc Chagall, the eldest of nine children, was born on 7 July 1887, into a family of Vitebsk Jews. The world of Eastern Jewry was both narrow and peaceful, going its quiet way between synagogue, fireside and shop (according to Chagall's own tongue-in-cheek account in *My Life*). Although only half of his hometown's population of 50,000 were Jews, Vitebsk had all the characteristic traits of the *shtetl*: wooden houses, a rural atmosphere, poverty. Thanks to his mother, Marc was enabled to go on to the official state school after he had finished at the *cheder*, the Jewish elementary school. Strictly speaking, Jews were not admitted to the state schools, but Feiga-Ita, enterprising woman that she was, bribed the teacher. So it was that Marc had the chance to escape the toils of neighbourly and nepotistic connections; instead of remaining trapped in humble confinement, he took violin and singing lessons, began to draw, and spoke Russian rather than Yiddish. Above all, he made contact with the bourgeois world where cosmopolitan and cultural interests were valued: a lifestyle that his father, Sachar, who sold herrings and was always weary, could never have offered him.

In the winter of 1906–07 the young Chagall moved to St Petersburg with his friend Viktor Mekler. In Vitebsk he had attended Yehuda Pen's art school, and now he was out for a thorough artistic training in the cultural heart of Russia. *Young Girl on a Sofa* (p. 8), a portrait of his sister Mariaska, which he painted on a visit home in 1907, is one of his earliest works and testifies to a newfound artistic confidence (which was vital in view of his family's scepticism).

"My father had blue eyes but his hands were covered in calluses. He worked, prayed, and kept his peace. Like him, I was silent too. What was to become of me? Was I to stay like that my whole life long, sitting by a wall, or would I haul barrels about, too? I took a look at my hands. My hands were too soft ... I had to find some special occupation, some kind of work that would not force me to turn away from the sky and the stars, that would allow me to discover the meaning of my life. Yes, that was what I was looking for. But in my home environment I was the only one who had ever uttered the words 'art' or 'artist'. 'What is an artist?', I asked."

MARC CHAGALL

OPPOSITE:
Red Nude Sitting Up, 1908
Oil on canvas, 90 x 70 cm (35½ x 27½ in.)
Private collection

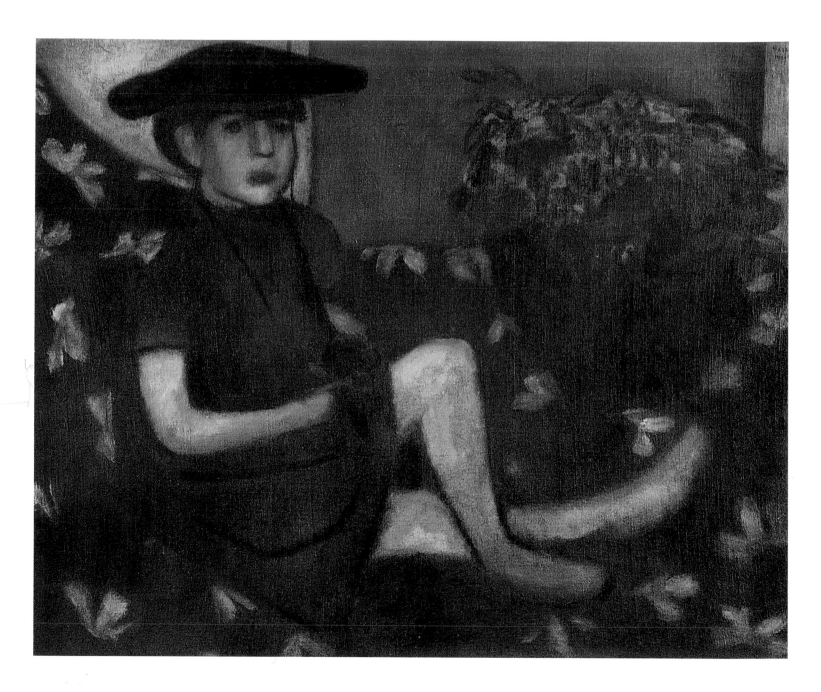

Young Girl on a Sofa (Mariaska), 1907
Oil on canvas, 72 x 92.7 cm (28¼ x 36½ in.)
Private collection

"With my 27 roubles in my pocket, the only money my father ever gave me for a journey, I disappear, still rosy-cheeked and curly-haired, to St Petersburg, accompanied by my friends. The die is cast."

MARC CHAGALL, in *My Life*

As if in a photograph, the girl is seen reclining on an outsize divan, legs coquettishly crossed, wearing a beret. Chagall's family were Orthodox Jews, but they were nevertheless willing to be photographed, and so this painting, with its everyday motifs and rather stiff pose, has something of the familiar and accepted air of camerawork. The decorative flatness, the blurred distinction between the figure and the blanket and the soft, rounded lines contouring the body reflect the influence of contemporary St Petersburg painting. None of this can quite conceal the technical weaknesses of the piece, however, particularly evident in Mariaska's limbs.

Red Nude Sitting Up (p. 6), painted a year later (also in Vitebsk), is a very different work, more powerful and of greater originality. Chagall had just won a scholarship to the celebrated Svanseva School where Léon Bakst taught, who was a major link with the West and an influential advocate of Symbolist painting. Bakst wrote for the periodical *Mir Iskusstva* (*The World of Art*). Through Bakst, Chagall acquired a finely tuned sense of his role as an artist and must have been helped towards new means of visual expression. In this new piece of work, the

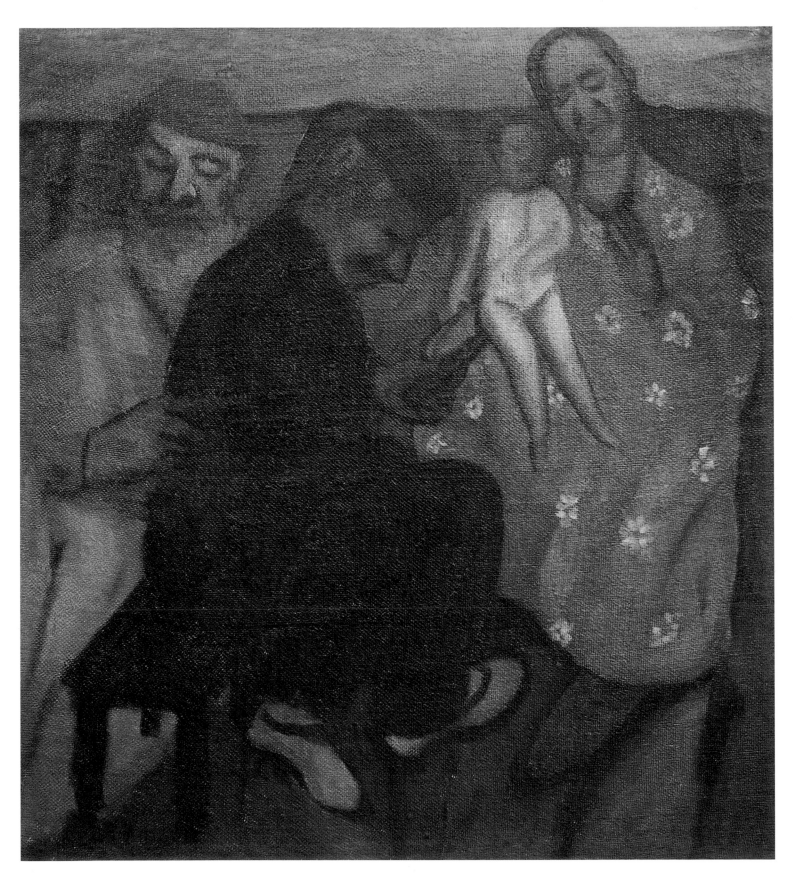

The Family, or Maternity, 1909
Oil on canvas, 74 x 67 cm (29 x 26½ in.)
Private collection

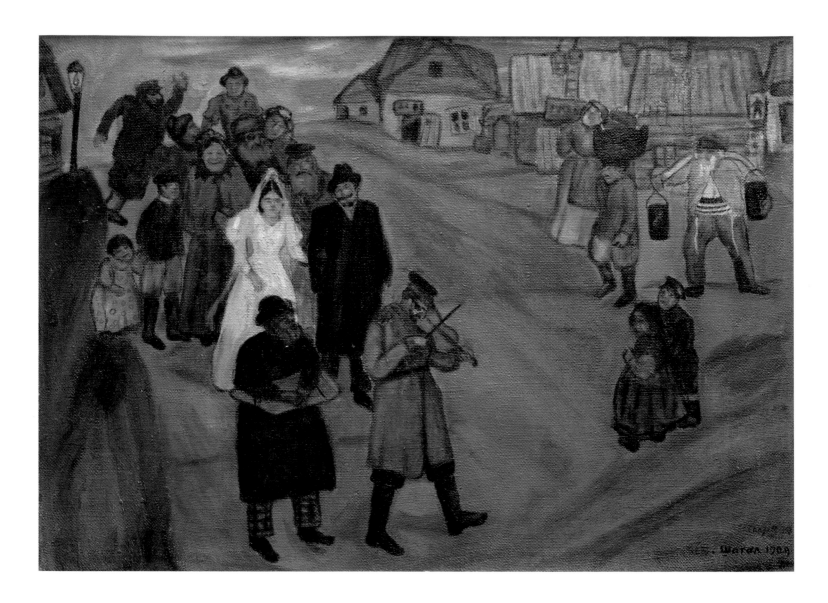

Russian Wedding, 1909
Oil on canvas, 68 x 97 cm (26¾ x 38¼ in.)
E.G. Bührle Collection, Zurich

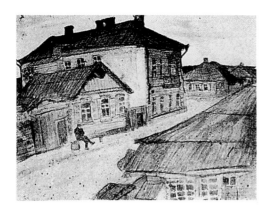

The Village Street, 1909
Pencil and gouache on paper,
28.8 x 38 cm (11¼ x 15 in.)
Private collection

artist shows his nude frontally and with a weighty, direct physicality that is quite unlike the *étude*-like reticence of the picture of Mariaska. The unconventional red shades and their contrast with the green of the plant suggest that Chagall was familiar with recent French painting, in particular with that of Henri Matisse, an impression that is confirmed by the fragmented rendering of the figure, making it torso-like and rapt.

Chagall was not the smug and lordly artist-prince he portrayed himself as in the *Self-Portrait with Brushes* (p. 2), where we see him gazing disrespectfully out of the picture. But by 1909 he was no longer a naïve lad either. Now, in his apprentice years in the capital, away from his origins among the simple folk of the provinces, Chagall was able to turn to the subjects and motifs that were to be typical of his future work: village scenes, peasant life, intimate views of a small world. Not until he sensed this contrast with his bohemian life in the big city, with its financial problems and the possibility of fame, did Chagall acquire his tender and loving eye for the life of the *shtetl*.

It is this tension that enriches the quality of another work of 1909, *The Family, or Maternity* (p. 9). The large areas, tranquil figures and simple gestures produce a monumental sense of dignity, translating everyday Jewish rituals into a timeless realm of iconic peacefulness. Compositionally, the painting derives from a traditional Western configuration of the circumcision of Christ with the high priest, Madonna and Child, with Joseph discreetly remaining in the background. Giving us the option of reading his painting allegorically by borrowing the formal arrangement of a Christian story for his everyday scene, Chagall preserves the ambiguity of his own artistic technique, which was midway between naïvety and symbolically gestural formality – much in the way that Paul Gauguin, his idol at that time, painted the Nativity in the South Seas.

Russian Wedding (left), on the other hand, appears to be a genre painting, but in fact reflects a happy development in Chagall's own private life. In autumn 1909, through Thea Bachmann, he became acquainted with Bella Rosenfeld, the daughter of a Jewish jeweller, who also came from Vitebsk and who was studying in Moscow. She too had left her original homeland. In 1915 she was to marry Chagall, and many of his paintings, which were dedicated to her, were to depict the special harmony of their relationship.

In *My Life* Chagall writes that he "... found the house full of serious men and women", "and the crowds of black figures dimmed the daylight. Noise, whispers, then suddenly the piercing cry of a new-born child. Mama, half-naked, lay in bed, pale, a tender pink. My youngest brother was seeing the light of the world." In 1910 Chagall worked up this scene into the painting *Birth* (below), a key work

"My name is Marc, my emotional life is sensitive and my purse is empty, but they say I have talent."
MARC CHAGALL, in *My Life*

Birth, 1910
Oil on canvas, 65 x 89.5 cm (25½ x 35¼ in.)
Kunsthaus, Zurich

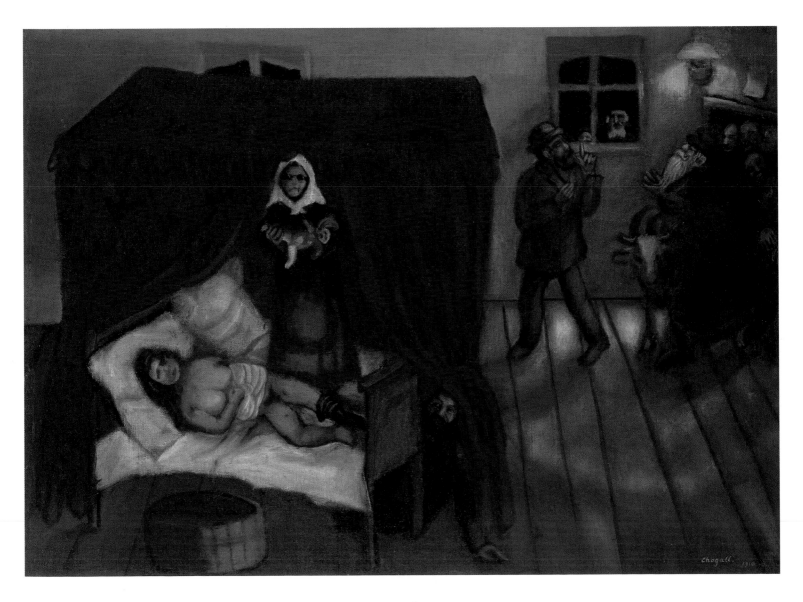

in the art of his early Russian years. With its dramatic lighting, the scene might be happening on a stage, and shows what Chagall had learnt from Bakst, who often designed stage sets. To the left we see the exhausted mother lying on the bed, the sheets heavily bloodstained, the impact heightened by the red canopy. The nurse, in hieratic posture, is holding the baby somewhat awkwardly. Beneath the bed crouches a bearded figure, maybe the father. From the right we see inquisitive neighbours and farmers shoving their way into the room (an old Jew is leading a cow) and others are looking in at the window.

The traditional cast of a Christian Nativity are here: the Holy Family, with herdsmen coming in to share in the event. But the artist has eliminated whatever the biblical tale offers in the way of anecdote, and indeed there is a strict structural division between the birth scene with the two women on the left, and the right side of the picture, where the men are mere onlookers. The personal experience described in *My Life*, the everyday event of birth and the allusion to the Christian motif, have all been integrated into a unifying structural principle that is fundamental and quite independent of any specific culture.

In *Birth* we see at its most ambitious Chagall's attempt, so characteristic of his early work, and well documented in his autobiography, to transcend conceptual boundaries and create new syntheses. But even if the visual logistics are clear and assured, the formal solution remains unsatisfying. The ideas are persuasive, but the picture falls apart into two halves. In his quest for an artistic language that might render the complexity of his conceptual insights, Chagall could no longer expect inspiration from Russian art, itself in its infancy. The only place to find answers was in the capital of the art world: Paris.

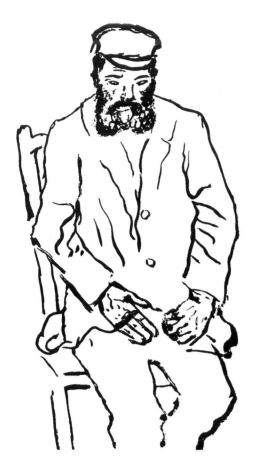

The Artist's Father, *c.* 1907
Indian ink and sepia, 23 x 18 cm (9 x 7 in.)
Private collection

"When I considered my father beneath his lamp I dreamt of skies and stars far from our street. All the poetry of life was in my father's sadness and silence, to my mind. There was the inexhaustible source of my dreams: my father, who could be compared to the immobile, secretive and silent cow that sleeps on the roof of the hut."

MARC CHAGALL

OPPOSITE:
Woman with a Bouquet, 1910
Oil on canvas, 64 x 53.5 cm (25¼ x 21 in.)
Private collection

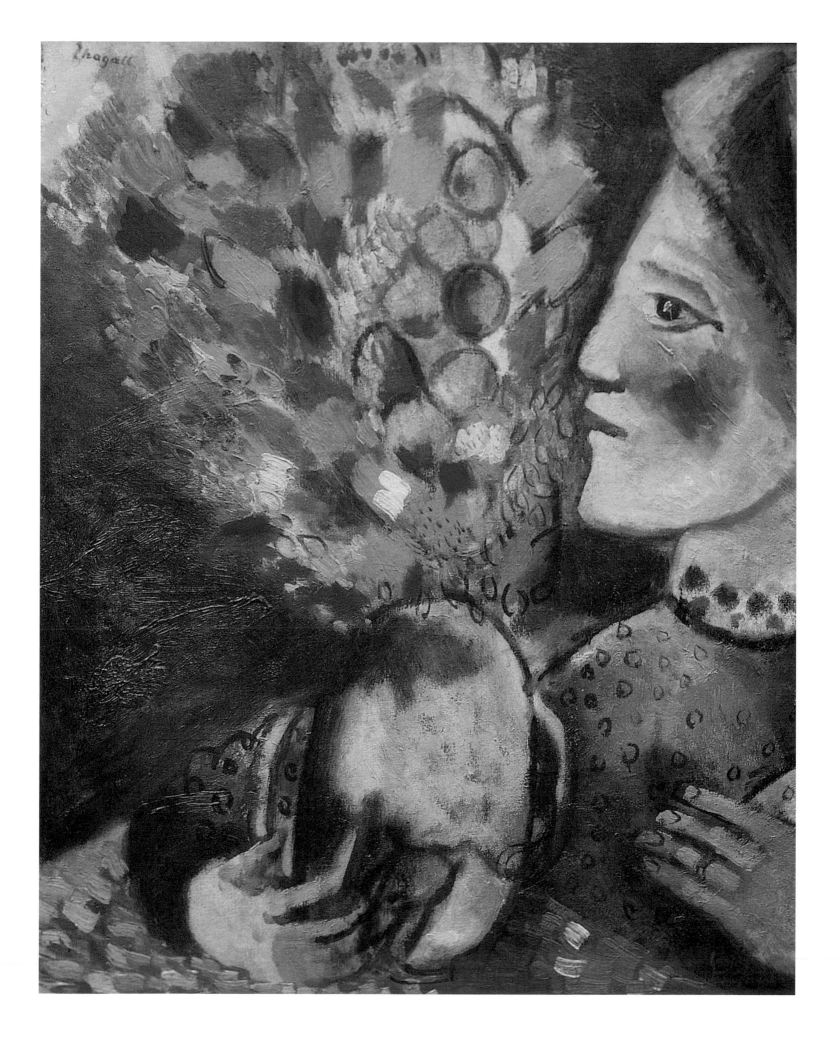

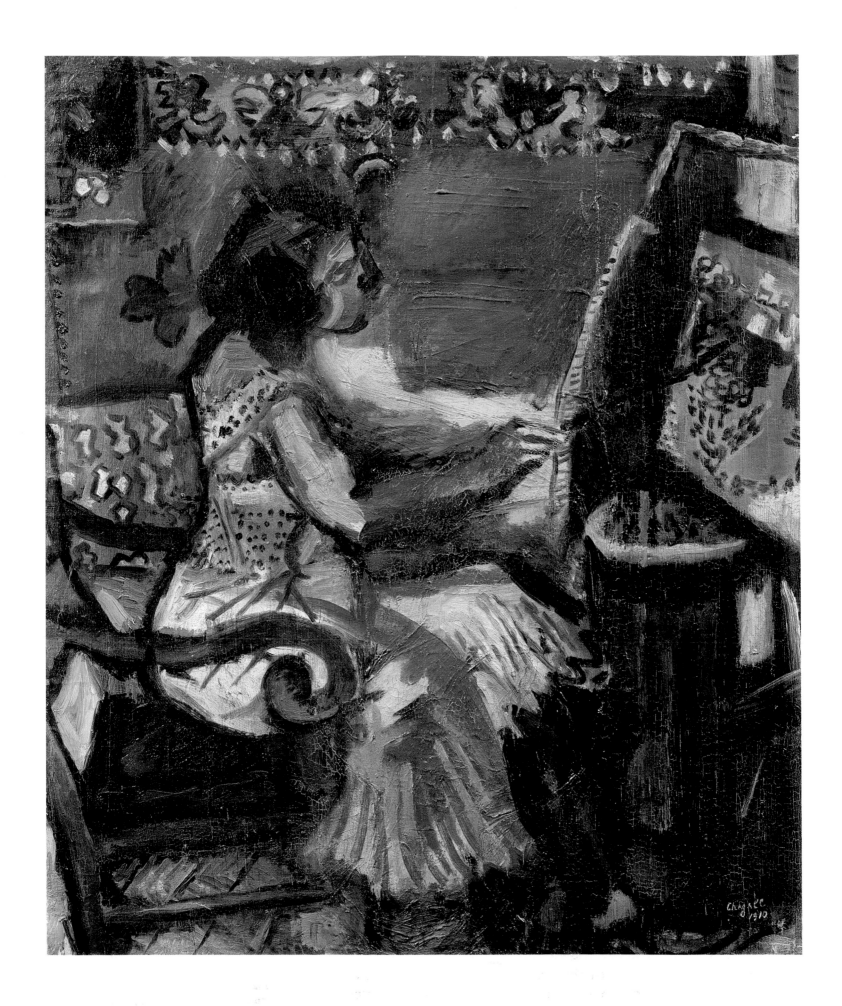

The Paris Years

1910–1914

Russia's young up-and-coming artists were likelier to be better received in Paris than in their own country. Sergei Diaghilev's Ballets Russes – the entire troupe of dancers, musicians, writers and painters – had scored a sensation there with their mixture of sublimity and exoticism and had awakened longings for the vast spaces of the East. Russia was "in". Alexei von Jawlensky, Vassili Kandinsky, Jacques Lipchitz, and all the artists who were to achieve worldwide fame, took advantage of the fashion to get to know Modernism at its place of birth. Bakst had arrived in 1909 to work with Diaghilev. In 1910 Chagall too made the four-day rail trip in the autumn, taking with him the spartan funds his St Petersburg patron, Max Winawer, allowed him and hopes of being supported by the numerous Russians living in Paris. He moved into his first studio in Montmartre, in a fellow Russian's flat.

"All that prevented me from returning immediately was the distance between Paris and my home town", Chagall writes in his memoirs, reflecting on the upheaval that had so unsettled this country-born artist. Indeed, the young Chagall was plunged into the world of art, seeing the Impressionists at Paul Durand-Ruel's, Gauguin and Vincent van Gogh at the Galerie Bernheim (the first time he had seen the original works), and the astonishing Matisse at the Autumn Salon. Above all, he discovered the Old Masters: "The Louvre put an end to my uncertainty." In paintings such as *The Model* (left), done soon after his arrival, we see his new engagement with the French artistic tradition. Chagall's palette, it is true, retains the earthy darkness of his Russian pictures, but the thick application of the paint and the frayed, fibrous juxtaposition of colourful brush-strokes reflect contemporary colour theories. Chagall's subject is a studio scene, and thus a meditation on his own work, but his model is holding a brush as well and painting a picture herself, which metaphorically creates an atmosphere of prevalent creativity, an artistic commitment that reaches into all aspects of everyday life. "Starting with the market, where I could only buy a piece of a cucumber since I had no money; through the worker in his blue overalls, to the keenest disciples of Cubism; everything testified to a definite sense of measure and clarity, a precise sense of form," writes Chagall, describing this creative flair. It was a flair he wanted to appropriate in his own work.

The artist did all that was in his power to promote the legend of his own poverty. Not only the cucumber he could only afford a piece of, not only the herring whose head he ate one day and tail the next, but even the very paintings he did in this early Paris period remind us of how poor Chagall was. Many of them are painted on canvas that had already been painted on and Chagall proved skilful

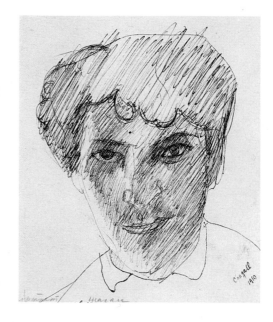

Self-Portrait, 1910
Pen and black Indian ink on paper,
14.7 x 13.1 cm (5¾ x 5¼ in.)
Musée national d'art moderne,
Centre Georges Pompidou, Paris

OPPOSITE:
The Model, 1910
Oil on canvas, 62 x 51.5 cm (24½ x 20¼ in.)
Private collection

15

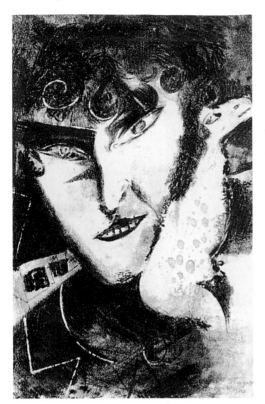

Self-Portrait with Goat, 1922–3
Lithograph, 41 x 26.4 cm (16 x 10½ in.)

"At that time I had grasped that I had to go to Paris. The soil that had nourished the roots of my art was Vitebsk; but my art needed Paris as much as a tree needs water. I had no other reason for leaving my homeland, and I believe that in my paintings I have always remained true to it."

MARC CHAGALL

OPPOSITE:
To My Betrothed, 1911
Gouache, oil and watercolour on paper,
61 x 44.5 cm (24 x 17½ in.)
Philadelphia Museum of Art, Philadelphia

at manipulating contrasts of light and dark, inherited through this re-use, for his own purposes of lighting. While the re-use of old canvases was good for demonstrating financial difficulties, in time it also became an expressive medium in its own right, and indeed a characteristic aesthetic procedure of the Cubists.

Interior II (p. 18), painted in 1911, shows us Chagall's first tentative ventures into Cubism. The Cubist idiom is seen in the angular shapes that mark the woman's skirt and the table edge, but beyond this seemingly abstract centre the picture also has a narrative content. In wild abandon, a woman is falling upon a bearded man and dragging a goat behind her. The man, who makes a fearful and defensive impression, cowering in his chair, is fending her off by grasping her thigh. The man's distress and the woman's instinctive wrath are conveyed by means of a centuries-old compositional trick by which, as in the reading process, we are made to interpret the dynamics of motion along a line from left to right.

In *To My Betrothed* (right), painted at the same time, Chagall evolved a more contemporary approach to the same subject, although in the treatment of sexuality this painting is once again archetypal. Here, the full vitality of the subject is developed (albeit the compositional structure is distinguished by its total tranquillity within the terms of the visual medium): the woman twines about the shoulders of the bull-headed man like a snake, spitting into his face, while the man, with every appearance of calmness, grasps at her leg with a gesture that suggests desire rather than defence. The tale and its symbolic content are inseparable. They have become this way not only through the unity of human and animal, but particularly through the woman's radial movement as well, a demonstration of power that seems impossible for the man to escape from. If *Interior II* could still be viewed as a harmless genre scene, that was no longer feasible now. Indeed, it was only after protracted argument that Chagall was allowed to exhibit this painting at the 1912 Spring Salon at all. He was accused of painting pornography. What gave this picture its bold suggestiveness was the simple compositional variation of arranging the motifs in circular form around a centre rather than stringing them in one linear direction. It was a procedure Chagall had learnt from Cubism. In fact, Cubism was to solve many of Chagall's early technical problems.

Chagall's link with Cubism was forged not so much by Pablo Picasso or Georges Braque, the movement's founding fathers, as by Robert Delaunay, who was married to the Russian painter Sonia Terk. The orthodox Cubists' coolly dissecting gaze was not the way Chagall and Delaunay looked at things, nor were they interested in the solitary dignity of concrete objects, which enabled the Cubists to make even painted canvas their subject. And the dichotomy of abstraction and representation, Braque's and Picasso's integral method by which ordinary scrutiny of a thing would be amplified by everyday available knowledge of its uses, was of secondary importance to them too. For Delaunay, and especially for Chagall, Cubism represented an artistic language for the expression of the world's magic, the secret life of things, beyond mere functionality. It provided them with geometrical patterns, models for ordering dreams, experiences, desires and visions, ways of re-creating them in terms of a visual logic that could be grasped by others. Imagined realities were complicated enough, needing an appropriate medium; and the Russian's visions, jostling for

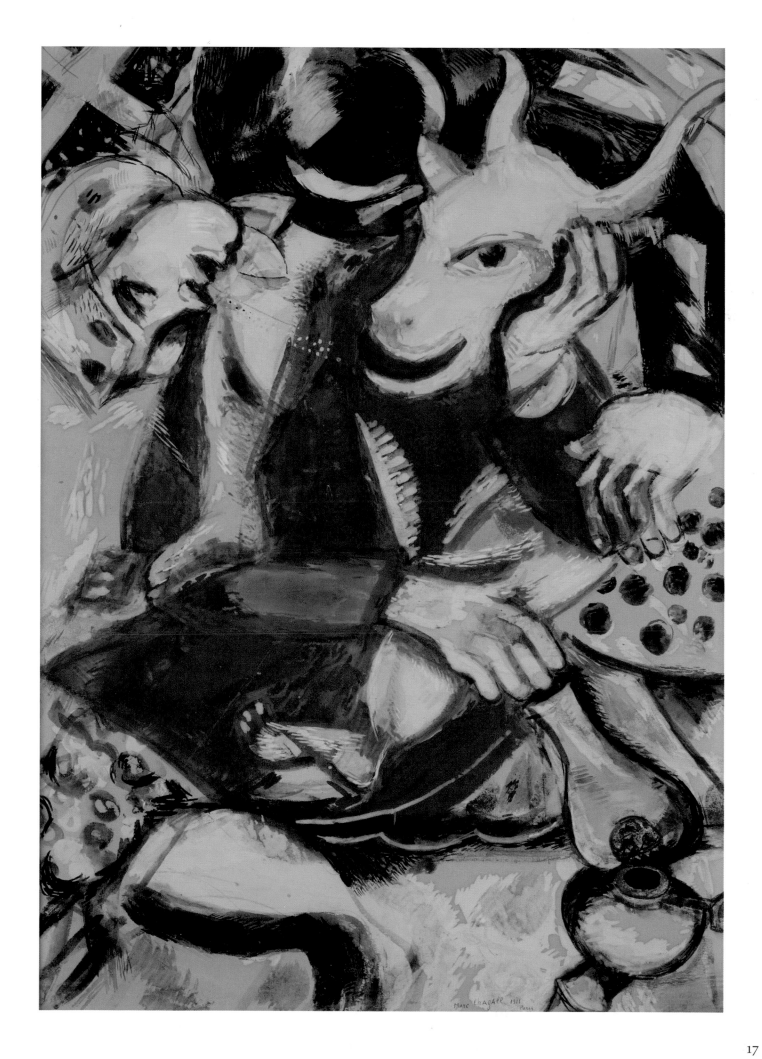

"In Paris I went to neither the art academy nor to the professors. The city itself was my teacher, in all things, every minute of the day. The market-folk, the waiters, the hotel porters, the farmers, the workers. They were enveloped in something of that astounding atmosphere of *lumière-liberté* ['enlightened freedom'] that I had never come across anywhere else."

MARC CHAGALL

Interior II, 1911
Oil on canvas, 100 x 180 cm (39½ x 70¾ in.)
Private collection

expression in his Paris years, found their needs answered by the complexity of Cubist forms.

Near the Paris abattoirs there was an artists' colony known as "La Ruche" ("The Beehive") because of the shape of its central building, a dodecagonal wooden pavilion. This was one of the places that gave Paris its reputation as an art metropolis; painters and sculptors from all over the world gathered there in quest of international careers. It had nearly 140 studios, rudimentary and dirty, but cheap; and in the winter of 1911–12 Chagall moved into one of them. His neighbours included a number of Russians, among them Chaim Soutine, a wilful and grouchy eccentric, an Eastern Jew like Chagall. With the move, a change occurred in the format of Chagall's works; he now had more space than his little quarters in Montmartre provided, and was able to paint on bigger canvases. Many of the pictures he did at La Ruche bear the date "1911", but in fact the artist did not date them immediately on completion, and when he did so later, looking back, he rather mixed up the chronological order of his works. For his own purposes, he grouped his oeuvre into cycles he then dated according to the promptings of some inner time-schedule, which had little to do with the realities of the calendar. This may seem a trivial point, but here, too, Chagall proves a master of ironic deception, affecting to despise conventions of orderliness and only conceding allegiance to a clownish inner world of his own.

I and the Village (p. 21) is dated "1911" but was painted at La Ruche; it is Chagall's definitive programmatic painting of the Paris years. The radial, centrifugal structure of the picture has here become the major compositional principle. Chagall starts out from Delaunay's use of sectional, sliced images – with the

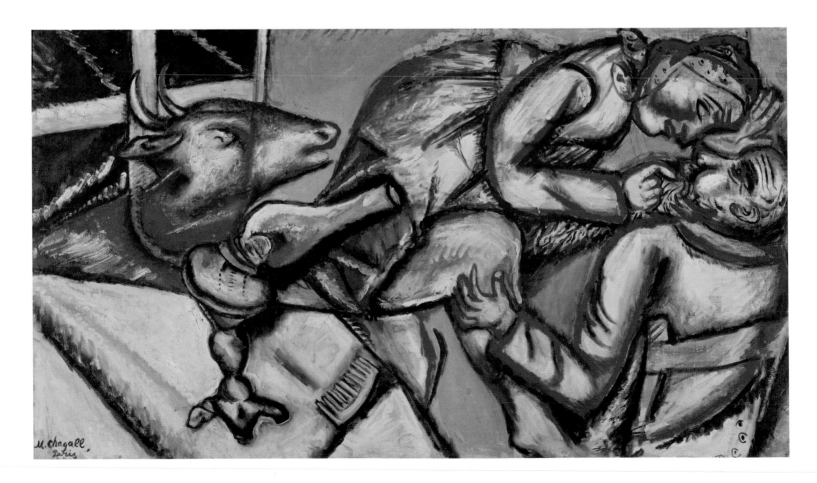

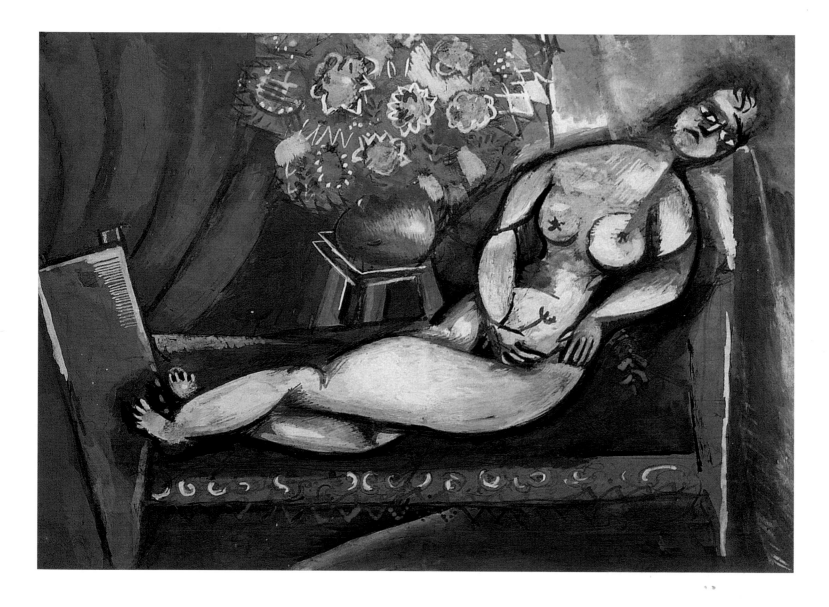

analogy of circle and sun as a figurative element in what is an otherwise abstract configuration of colour – and goes on to achieve a pictorial unity through the yoking of motifs taken from different realms of given reality. The four sections of the work are dominated by archetypal human and animal figures as well as Nature (in the form of a twig) and Civilization (the village). Narration and plot are no longer needed; the geometrical arrangement, criss-crossing the picture with diagonals and arcs, suffices to give order to the subject. Two of Cubism's most electrifying devices, the juxtaposition of motifs and a certain transparency in the forms, are tested here for their ability to realize images from memory as well as visions and fragments of the most diverse kinds of reality in a painting. The head of the lamb, its contours creating the space for the milking scene, houses and people standing on their heads, and proportions contrary to all experience, are arranged on associative lines and stand for a reality beyond the visible world, for an imaginative realm in which memories become symbols. For, indeed, all the details in *I and the Village* are taken from memory. The artist has availed himself of Cubism, which places so strong an emphasis on concrete appearance, in order to create an autonomous world dependent on nothing but his own psychology. "Once in Paris I was finally able to express the (somehow) culinary joy I had sometimes felt in Russia – the joy of my childhood memories of Vitebsk," writes Chagall. Not until he was in Paris did he find the means to

Reclining Nude, 1911
Gouache on cardboard,
24 x 34 cm (9½ x 13½ in.)
Private collection

"There in the Louvre, looking at paintings by Manet, Millet and others, I realized why my links to Russia and Russian art were so slack, why I did not even speak their language."
MARC CHAGALL, in *My Life*

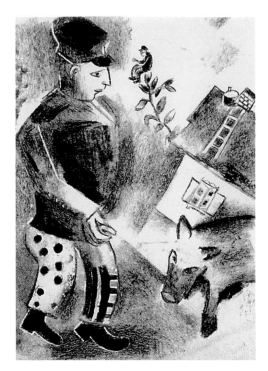

The Man with the Pig, 1922–3
Lithograph, 46.5 x 32.5 cm (18¼ x 12¾ in.)

OPPOSITE:
I and the Village, 1911
Oil on canvas, 192.1 x 151.4 cm (75½ x 59½ in.)
Museum of Modern Art, Mrs Simon
Guggenheim Fund, New York

open up his own inner world, his feelings of happiness, his longing for the little realm of his childhood.

The title *I and the Village* is notable for its imaginative succinctness, at odds (as it were) with the interplay of ambiguities in the painted scene. Like *To My Betrothed* (p. 17) or *To Russia, with Asses and Others* (p. 25), the title was thought out by Blaise Cendrars, Chagall's most important companion during the Paris years. Compared to the distinctly rigorous intellectuality of his fellow painters, the evocative staccato of images and the anarchic merriness of the linguistic coinages in Cendrars's poems and novels represented a counterpart to Chagall's associative world of wonders. Those who supported Chagall in his chosen approach, sharing his taste for poetry and likewise questing for the hidden significance of things, were literary people. "A genius, as split as a peach," Cendrars said of his friend. Chagall riposted with *Half Past Three (The Poet)* (p. 23). The poet is seen sitting alone at a table. Coffee cup in hand, a tempting bottle of brandy at his side, he seems to be in the throes of poetic inspiration. At all events he inhabits some imaginary, supernatural world: his head, his spirit, free of the body, even beyond the grid of diagonals that the world of images is contained in.

This homage to coffee-house literati shows Chagall already in the process of moving on beyond Cubism and the geometrical manner. The interwoven lines had previously merely served to achieve a sense of order; now they appear as an integral part of the painting's statement, enveloping the figure of the poet and, by emphasizing the freedom of the head, underlining the independence of the power of inspiration. Chagall was out to appropriate the imaginative strength of the poet and his independence of the principle of order. His geometrical structures abruptly became metaphors, the major bearers of poetic meaning.

Guillaume Apollinaire called Chagall's pictorial worlds "*surnaturel*"; later he was to call them "surreal". This concept, as "Surrealism", was to give a name to an era. The inventor of the term, Apollinaire, was not so much Chagall's friend as his mentor, and tirelessly tried to organize exhibition space for him. Chagall paid his thanks to him too, in *Homage to Apollinaire* (p. 26), although perhaps in this painting the artist somewhat too ambitiously plays with the aura of the mysterious stranger that Apollinaire had seen him as. At the centre of the composition (the circular shape matches the hint of a numbered dial) we see Adam and Eve with the apple, the two figures represented as one. Alongside this hermaphroditic image there is a dedicatory inscription with the names of friends and linguistic symbols of the four elements. Chagall's own signature also appears in cryptic form, stripped of vowels and with a cabbalistic air. This rather mysterious mixture of various secret doctrines no doubt satisfied Chagall's wish for an art that would draw upon many cultures; but it can communicate only with the help of words, and in that respect its method is closer to poetry than to painting.

"I do not personally believe that scientific aims serve the cause of art well. Impressionism and Cubism are alien to me. It seems to me that art is first and foremost a condition of the soul." Chagall's works increasingly reflected this unease concerning the neutral beauty of the visible world (here expressed to Apollinaire) and his rejection of "an era that sings hymns to technology and deifies Progress". Paintings such as *Adam and Eve* (p. 29), dated 1912, which still – with their dissectional analysis of form – owe everything to a sense of the intrinsic dynamics of shapes in art, prove typical for only a short period in

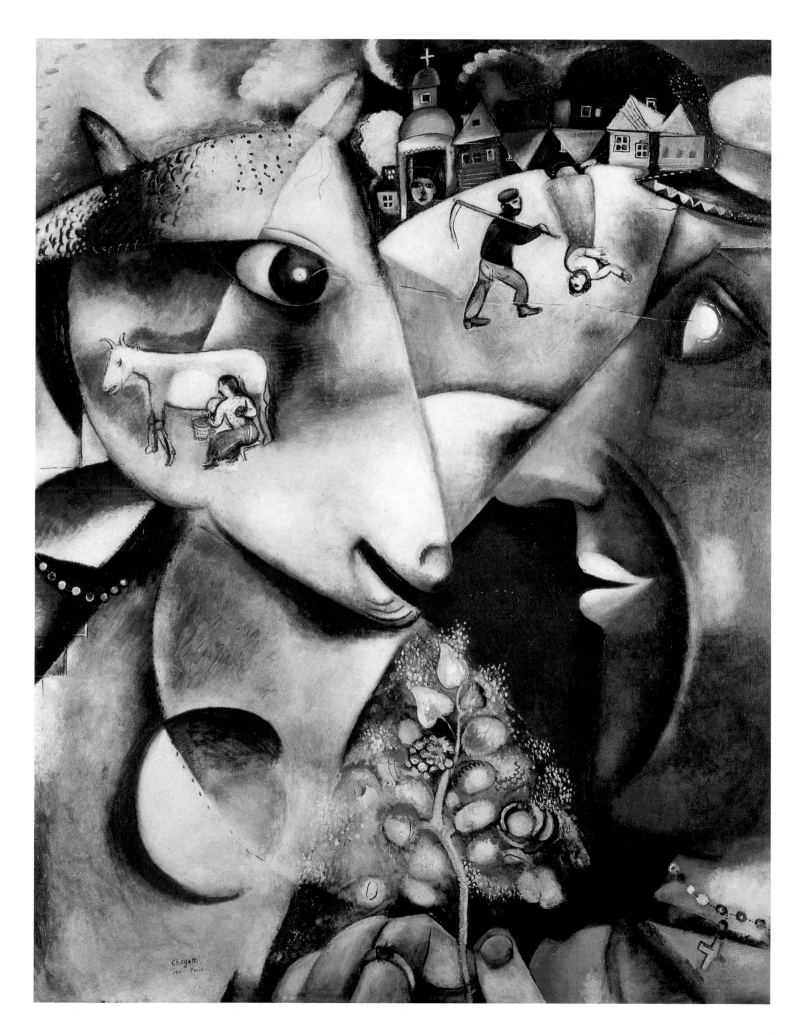

Marc Chagall

"He is asleep
Now he is awake
And suddenly he is painting
He reaches for a church paints with a church
He reaches for a cow and paints with a cow
With a sardine
With skulls hands knives
Paints with the nerves of an ox
All the besmirched sufferings of little Jewish towns
Tormented by burning love from the depth of
Russia
For France
Death heart and desires
He paints with his thighs
Has his eyes in his behind
There it is
Your face
It is You, dear reader
It is I
It is he
His own betrothed
The grocer on the corner
The milkmaid
Midwife
New-born babies are being washed
  in buckets of blood
Heavenly madness
Mouths gush forth fashions
The Eiffel Tower is like a corkscrew
Hands heaped on each other
Christ
He himself Jesus Christ
He lived a long youth on the cross
Every new day another suicide
And suddenly he is no longer painting
He was awake
Now he is asleep
Strangles himself with a tie
Chagall astonished
Borne on by immortality."

BLAISE CENDRARS

OPPOSITE:
Half Past Three (The Poet), 1911
Oil on canvas, 196 x 145 cm (77¼ x 57 in.)
Philadelphia Museum of Art, Philadelphia

Chagall's work. Soon his gaze returned in childishly naïve manner to the magic of the world, and he resumed his adventurous quest for the secrets told by things. The childhood experiences Chagall retells in his visual world are presented within the traditions of his origins as well as the anti-rational patterns of Russian thought and the strict veto on images that marked Jewish life. To this extent, Chagall's settings are never separable from a mystical, conceptual world where his motifs are transmuted into symbols that stand for some invisible reality.

The second version of *Birth*, dated 1912, indeed reveals a far freer sense of access to the mysteries of Nature (p. 28). The stiff pathos of the earlier version, where Chagall's desire for an artistic image impaired the expressive potential of the work, has gone, to be replaced by a cheerful acceptance of the story-telling urge. The young mother is still lying on her bloodstained sheets, but now she is surrounded by busy and colourful vitality: two women are conducting an excited conversation, others have nodded off at the stove, and to the right of the picture people are waiting to begin celebrating the happy event in a fit manner. The dynamics of visual shapes, introduced into Chagall's work by his borrowings from Cubism, adds a liveliness to the pictorial narrative. At last the childhood experiences that Chagall always made use of in his work have a vibrancy and charming vitality, which – quite apart from any symbolic values – renders them accessible in the simplest of ways as an account of life. The poet's head askew on his shoulders and the soldier, holding his finger under the *samovartap* and saluting, while his cap raises itself (as in *The Soldier Drinks*, p. 27), are often to be seen in this period of his oeuvre. The chatty tone is typical of Chagall.

As in the work of his great contemporary, Picasso, there are analytic and synthetic phases in alternation in Chagall's art. In the early Paris period, influenced by the analogous methods being applied by Cubism, Chagall explored his experiences through the interaction of motifs; he juxtaposed impressions and memories, linking them only by means of an abstract structure unifying the whole canvas space. Later in Paris he increasingly paid attention to the scene that dominated an entire picture, intensifying thought into one single moment where time appears to stand still. "Even as I was taking part in that unique upheaval in artistic techniques in France, in my own thoughts, in my soul as it were, I returned to my own country. I lived with my back turned to what was in front of me." Thus the artist described his focus on the past, writing in 1960; that return to the past was also a withdrawal from the art scene of the avant-garde, which equated artistic progress with novelty and with originality of language, both spoken or written.

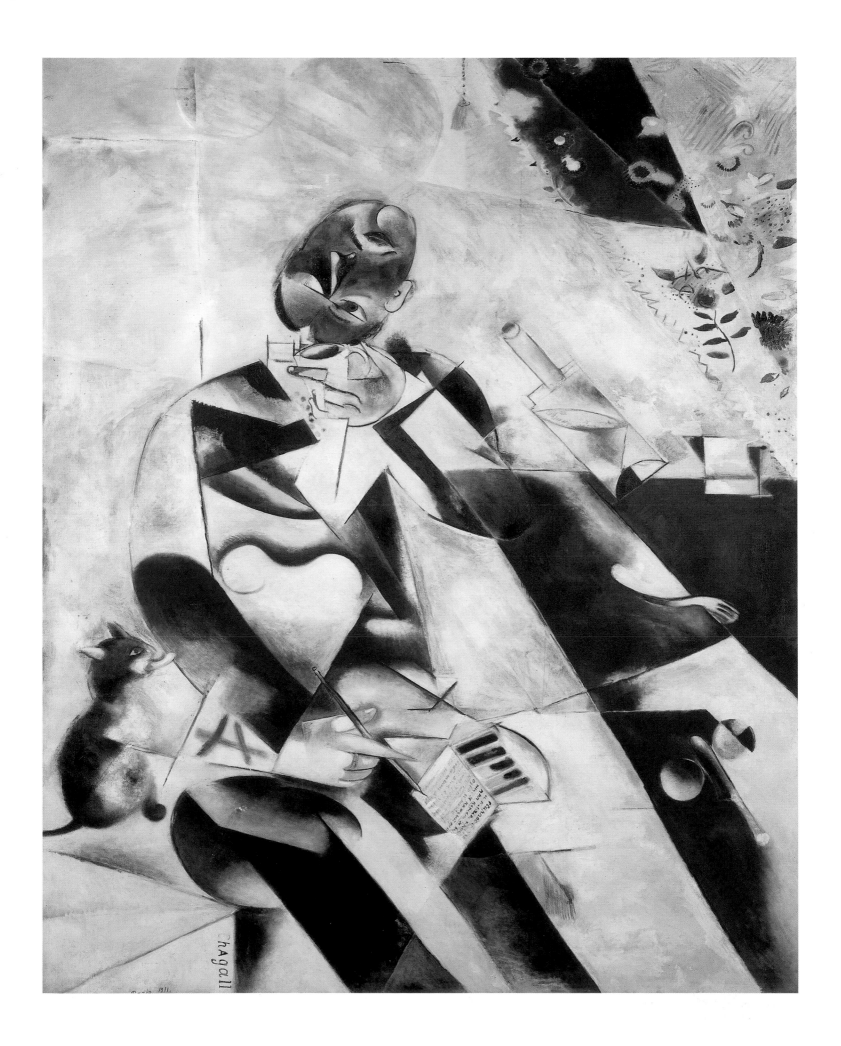

OPPOSITE:
To Russia, with Asses and Others, 1911
Oil on canvas, 157 x 122 cm (61¾ x 48 in.)
Musée national d'art moderne, Centre Georges Pompidou, Paris

The Cattle Dealer (p. 31), dated 1912 but (like so many of Chagall's paintings) probably done later, reproduces instead the harmonious simplicity of peasant life. Metaphors of security and well-being dominate this rural scene: the unborn foal in the mare's belly, the lamb on the woman's shoulders (alluding to the Christian image of the Good Shepherd), the bridge across which the cart is quietly rolling. The relaxed overall impression, created by the compositional sequence of horizontals and verticals, might lead us to forget that these animals also mean the money deals of the market-place; perhaps they are on their way to be slaughtered. Recollections of his homeland gave Chagall's portrayal something of the harmless prettiness of genre painting. *The Pinch of Snuff* (p. 30) pays still more striking homage to the homeland. The imperious figure of the bearded, side-locked Jew, with phylactery and Star of David in the background and the book with Hebrew characters, call up a familiar image, while the colours give it the defamiliarized appearance of a vision. It is caught between near and far, everyday and mystic, and testifies eloquently to the artist's homesickness. The book's Hebrew lettering includes the name "Segal Mosche", the artist's own name in his home country, a name that he had internationalized, for the sake of convenience, into "Marc Chagall" when still in Russia. His wish to see the homeland once more was growing ever stronger.

In spring 1914 he got his chance. At Apollinaire's suggestion, Herwarth Walden, mentor of the Expressionists and editor of *Der Sturm*, Germany's most significant avant-garde art periodical, arranged Chagall's first major solo exhibition at his Berlin gallery. Although he had sold a few graphic works, Chagall had been doing bad business in Paris, so the famous dealer's offer seemed tantamount to an international breakthrough. The irony of fate and politics decreed, however, that Chagall was to see none of the proceeds from these pictures. The outbreak of the First World War put his career back by years. "My paintings were showing off in the Potsdamer Strasse," Chagall recalled, "while nearby the cannons were being loaded." None the less, on 13 June 1914, he travelled to Russia on a visitor's visa, which was valid for three months, to attend his sister's wedding, revive memories and see Bella again. Soon frontiers were closed, and a stay he had meant to last weeks became one of eight years. Chagall had returned to the scene of almost all his paintings. *The Fiddler* (p. 33) is one of his last Paris works. The earlier version (p. 32), dated 1912–13, allows the table-cloth it is painted on to

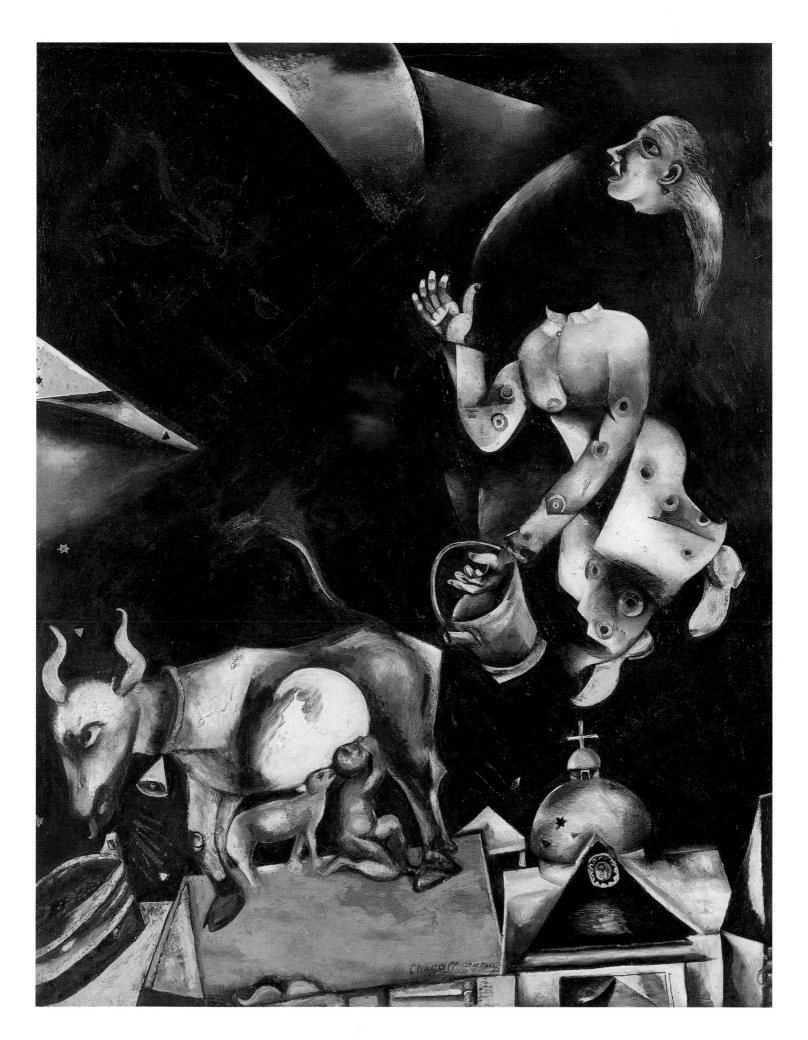

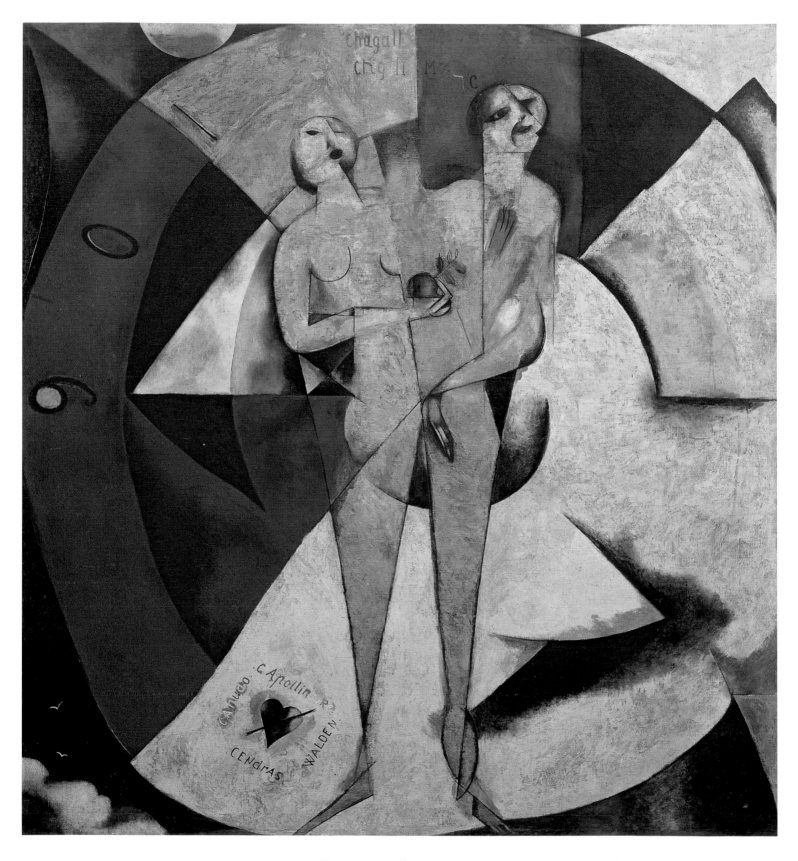

Homage to Apollinaire, 1911–12
Oil and powdered gold and silver on canvas, 200 x 189.5 cm (78¾ x 74½ in.)
Stedelijk van Abbe Museum, Eindhoven

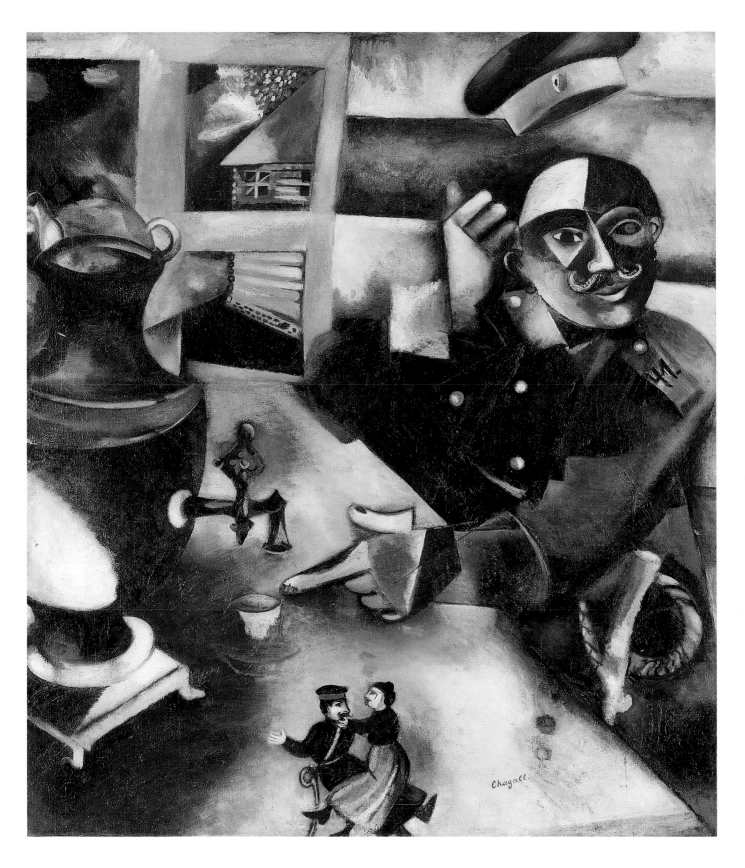

The Soldier Drinks, 1911–12
Oil on canvas, 109 x 94.5 cm (43 x 37¼ in.)
Solomon R. Guggenheim Museum, New York

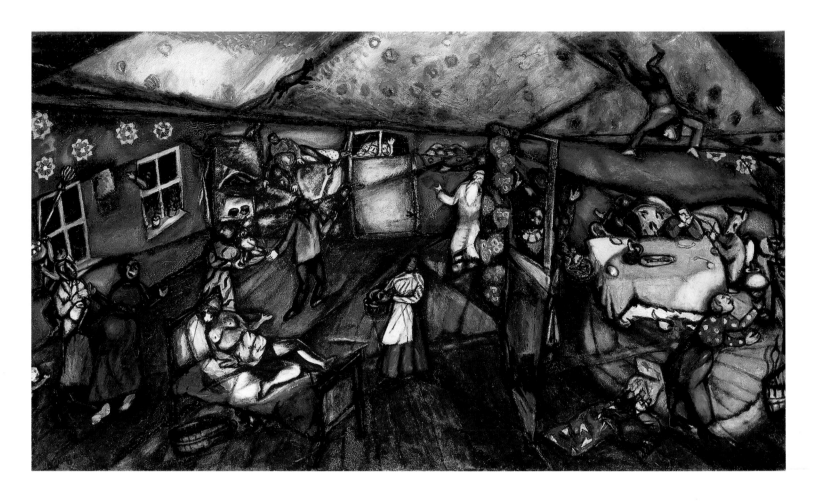

Birth, 1911
Oil on canvas, 113¼ x 195¼ cm (44½ x 76¾ in.)
Art Institute of Chicago, Chicago, Gift of Mr
and Mrs Maurice E. Culberg

show through, and in this, and in the use of mutually contradictory proportions, is squarely within the Cubist ambit; in the later version, by contrast, a twisty track curves through the canvas, lending the scene spatial and dramatic unity. The red-clad fiddler, with the beggar-lad behind him, is the dominant figure. Traditionally he leads Jewish wedding processions (compare the illustration on p. 10); we can therefore see the two people in the background as a newly-wed couple. The weighty equilibrium is scarcely disturbed any more by grotesqueness, and only the use of colour preserves those elements of the imagination that (of course) these pictures, painted in the great Western metropolis, in fact represent. *The Fiddler* tends to obscure its own artifice and effects a verisimilitude of the portrayed elements, despite the fact that they were not painted from life. Whatever the case, the painting includes expressive approaches that Chagall, with the motifs now immediately before him in Russia, would be able to re-use unchanged.

OPPOSITE:
Adam and Eve, 1912
Oil on canvas, 160.5 x 109 cm (63½ x 43 in.)
St Louis Art Museum, St Louis

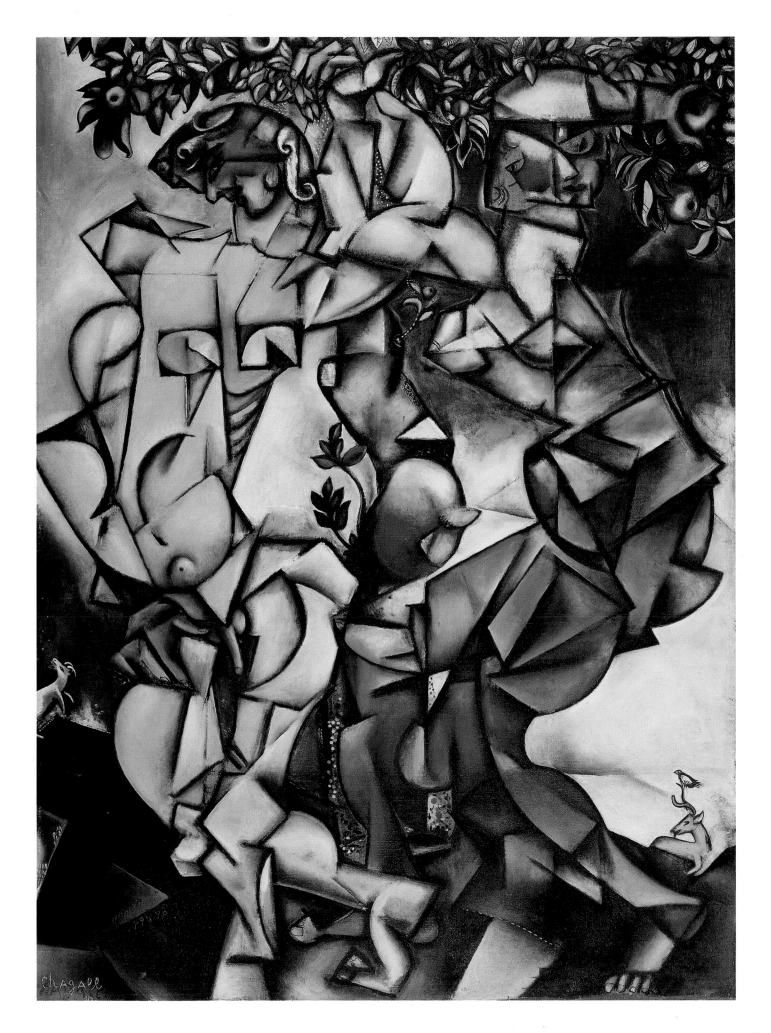

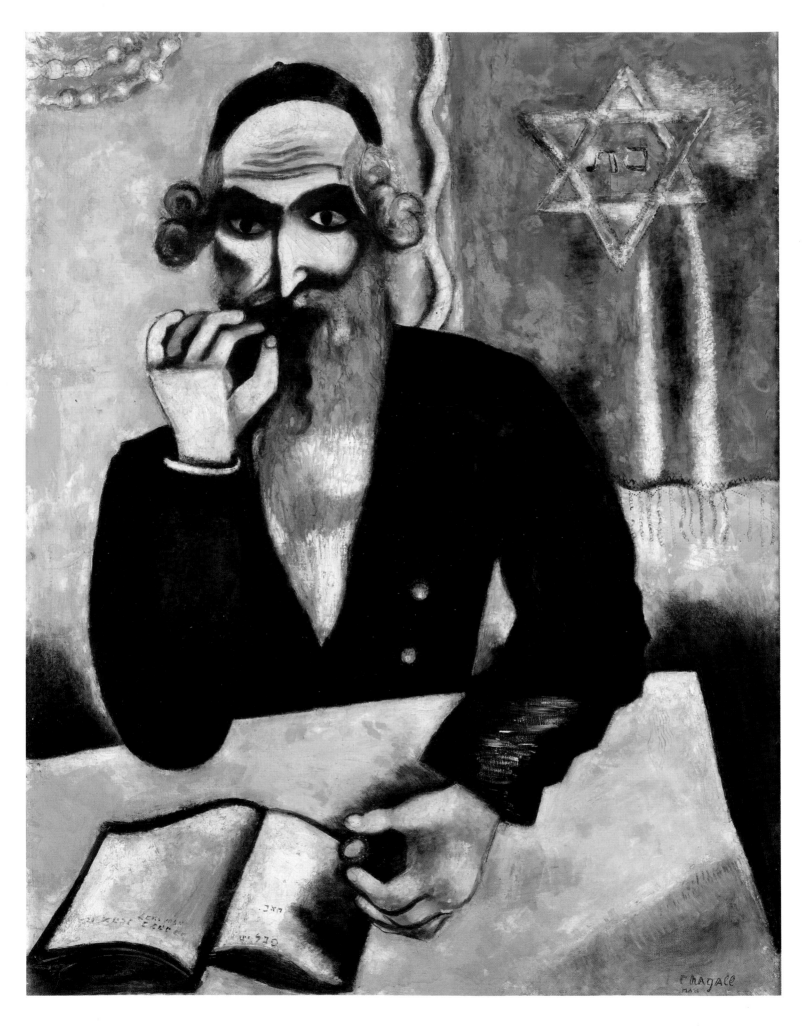

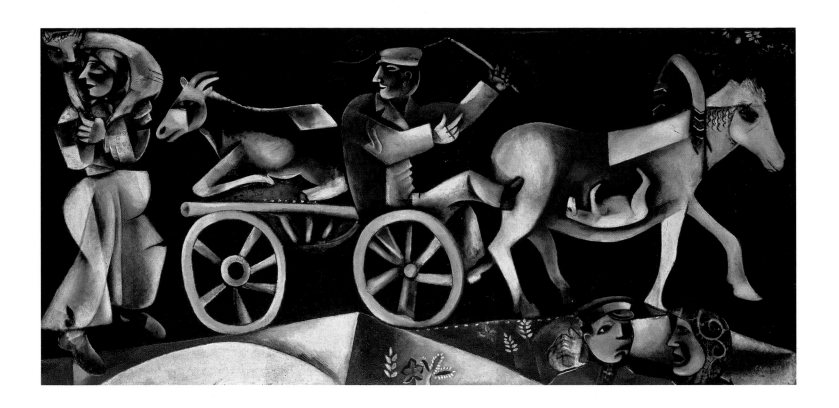

The Cattle Dealer, 1912
Oil on canvas, 97 x 200.5 cm (38¼ x 79 in.)
Kunstmuseum, Basle

OPPOSITE:
The Pinch of Snuff, 1912
Oil on canvas, 128 x 90 cm (50½ x 35½ in.)
Private collection

PAGE 32:
The Fiddler, 1912–13
Oil on canvas, 188 x 158 cm (74 x 62¼ in.)
Stedelijk Museum, Amsterdam

PAGE 33:
The Fiddler, 1911–14
Oil on canvas, 94.5 x 69.5 cm (37¼ x 27½ in.)
Kunstsammlung Nordrhein-Westfalen, Düsseldorf

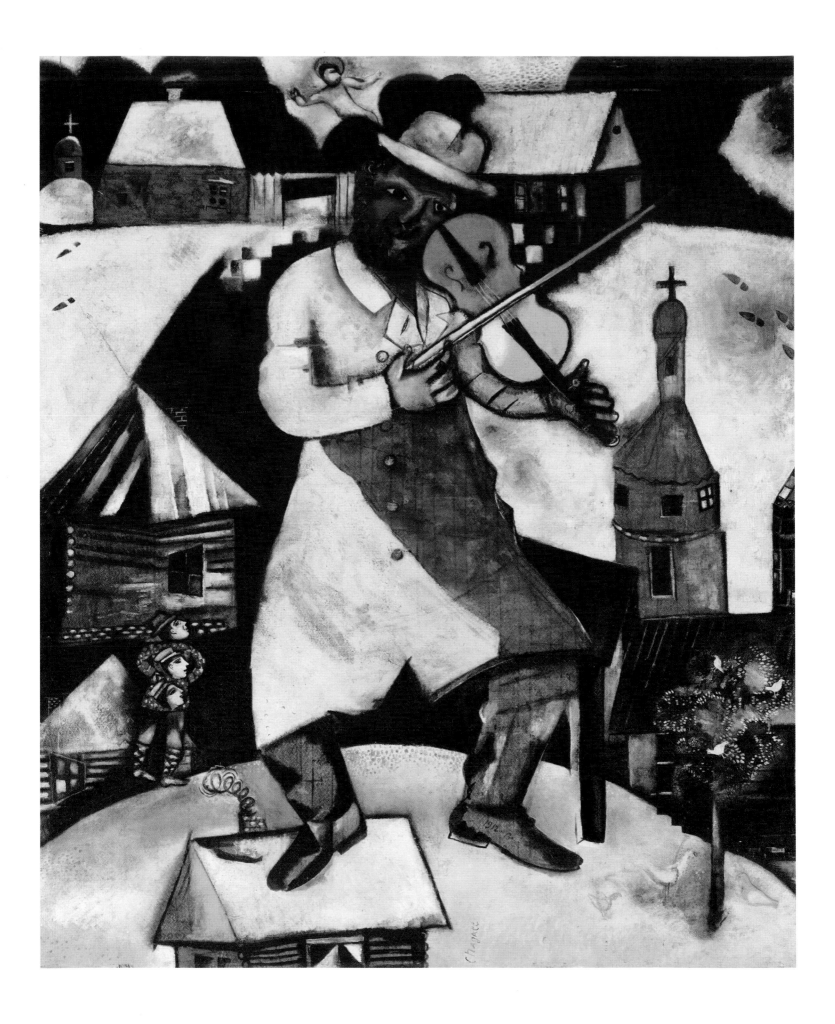

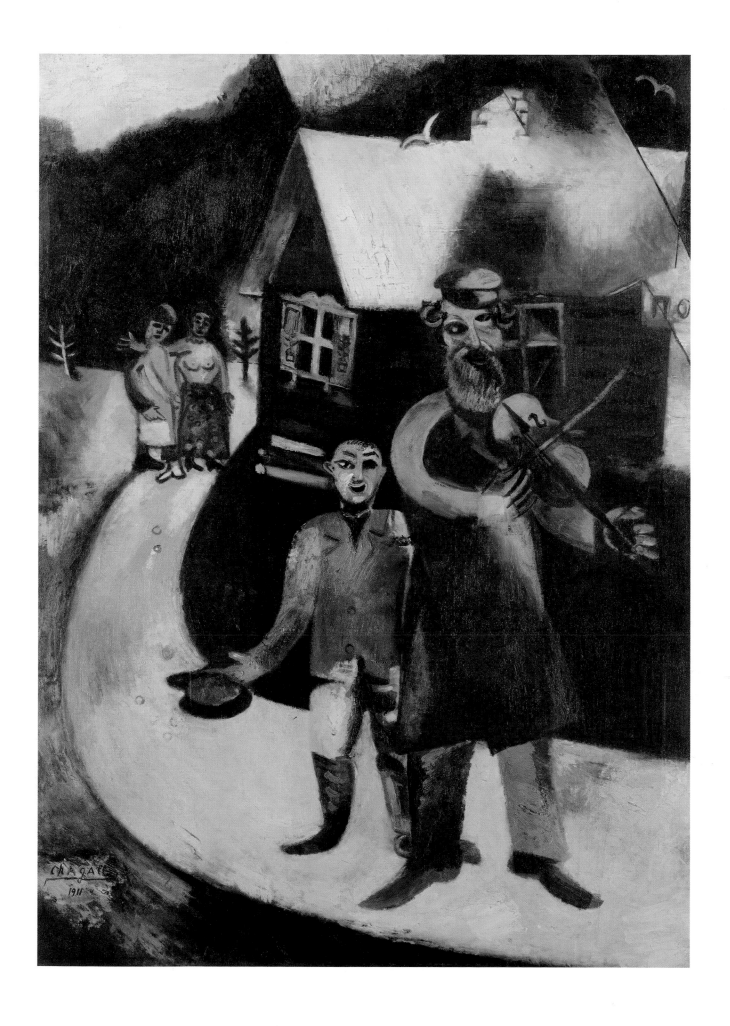

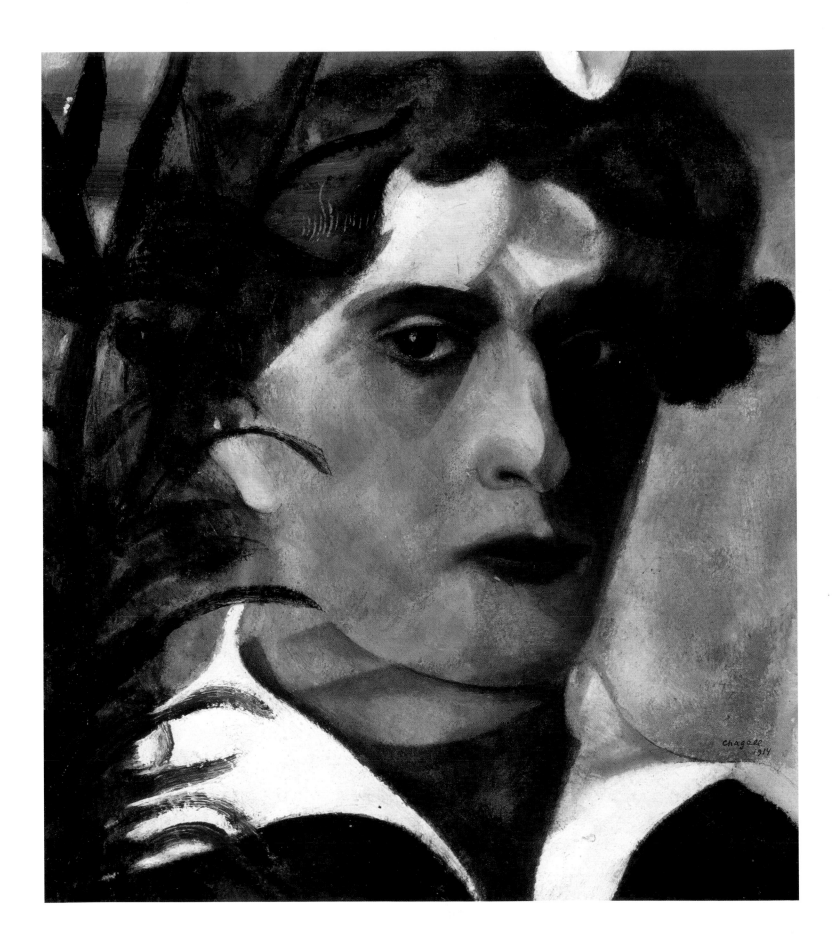

War and Revolution in Russia

1914–1923

"Vitebsk is a world all of its own, a unique town, an unhappy town, a boring town." Still, compared with what Chagall was to experience in the years ahead, his adjective "boring" might be better applied to Paris than to his home town. His stay in France was marked by constant work and the uneventful social life of elite bohemian circles. His Paris work was inspired less by an attempt to grasp the reality of the big city than by reflection on himself, a quest for the sources of his own vitality. Now, war and revolution were to determine Chagall's life – and his art, too – and were to place him in situations of considerable existential trouble.

All pretentiousness has disappeared from the self-portrait he painted shortly after his return (left). The artist now shows us a changed man, compared to the similar version done in 1909 (p. 2); sceptically, almost with a touch of mystery, he peers out from the leaves of the plant, ready to hide behind them at any moment. Here Chagall emphasizes the soft, feminine features of his face. He has something of the little boy smearing rouge on his face (as he used to like doing). No doubt this painting may have corresponded to what his family expected to see, may have confirmed the image of him that had remained with them. More than that, however, the portrait documents Chagall's fear of conscription into the Czar's army. Chagall vehemently avoids even the remotest suggestion of manly strength that might have made him a kind of wartime cannon-fodder (as Jews at that time had often been regarded).

Woina ("war") is the sole word we can make out on the front page of *The Smolensk Newspaper* (p. 37). The paper is on the table between two men, whose conversation appears to deal exclusively with the carnage ahead of Europe. The old Jew, resting his chin thoughtfully in his cupped hands, is thinking of the compulsory conscription Czarist regimes have been imposing on his people from time immemorial. Nor is his vis-à-vis, whose suit and hat pronounce him to be a bourgeois, at all enthusiastic either; he is seen mopping his brow in distraction.

Paul Cézanne's *Card Players* influenced this painting, but Chagall is in no mood for the harmless games depicted by the French artist. What the painting expresses is trepidation and consternation. He cannot bring himself to utter the loud "hooray" that many of his fellow artists (such as Apollinaire) shouted as they went to war. "Did you see the old man praying? That is he. It would be wonderful to be able to work in peace like that. At times a figure stood before me, a man so old and tragic that he already looked like an angel. But I could not stand to be near him for longer than half an hour. He stank too terribly."

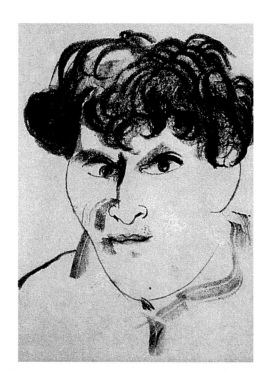

Self-Portrait, 1922–3
Lithograph, 24.5 x 18.2 cm (9½ x 7¼ in.)

OPPOSITE:
Self-Portrait, 1914
Oil on cardboard, 30 x 26.5 cm (11¾ x 10½ in.)
Philadelphia Museum of Art, Philadelphia

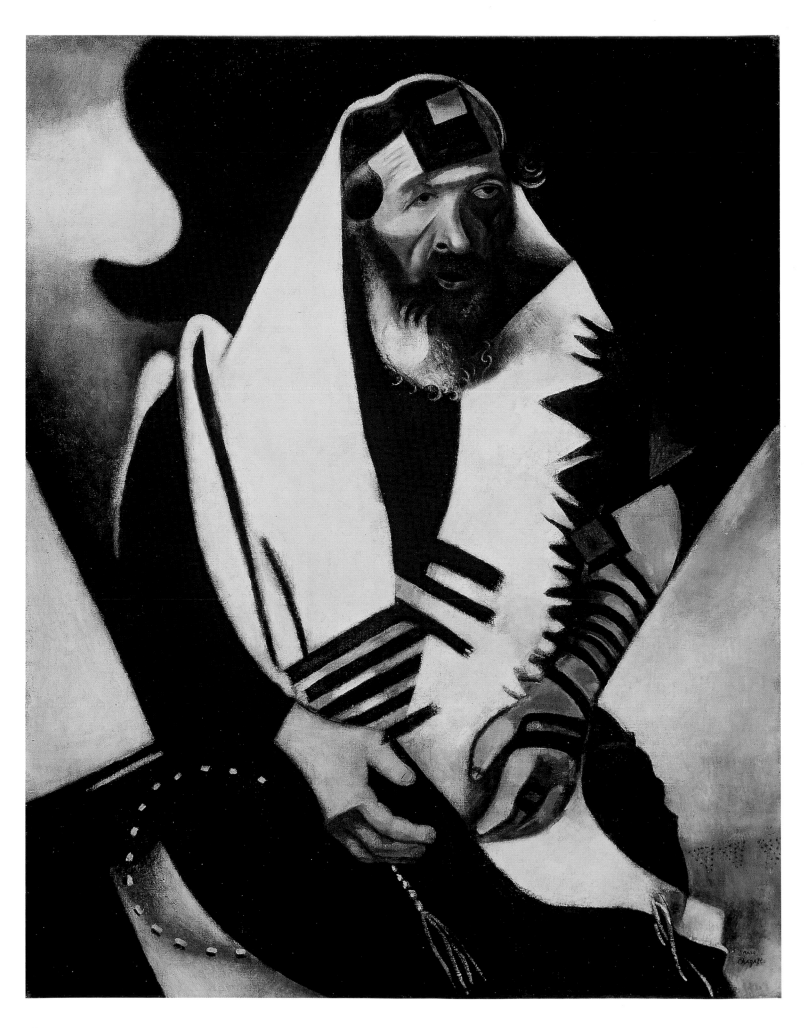

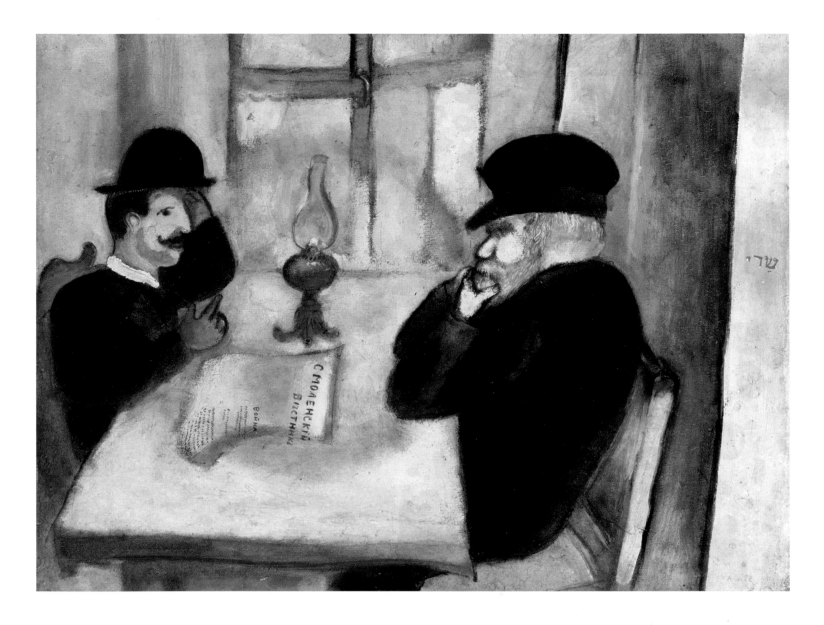

Affectionately, jokingly, and with the urbane nonchalance of a man of the world, Chagall approached the small world he had grown up in, and out of. Paintings such as *The Praying Jew (Rabbi of Vitebsk)* (left) or *Feast Day (Rabbi with Lemon)* (p. 39) readily rely on the immediate charm of the subjects and the timeless dignity we sense in these old and superannuated servants of the faith. Yet at the same time, it is plain that Chagall is critical of their attachment to an idyll that the artist can no longer share. These paintings are the icons of a latter time.

On 25 July 1915, Chagall married Bella, whom for many years he had loved at a long distance. There were problems, above all the grudges borne by Bella's parents, who had hoped their son-in-law would be of a better family. But their reservations were dispelled – at the latest, nine months later (almost to a day), when little Ida was born. In times of confusion, the young couple were in the seventh heaven, and *The Birthday* (p. 38) testifies to their happiness. Chagall has painted the pattern on the sofa cushion with minute attention, and the table-cloth too; in all things he is at pains to reproduce the furnishings of the room exactly. The love to which this picture attests has a concrete setting and is no mere vision of the beloved (as used to be the case in Paris), but really exists. "All I had to do was open my window," writes Chagall, "and in streamed the

The Smolensk Newspaper, 1914
Oil on paper on canvas, 38 x 50.5 cm (15 x 20 in.)
Philadelphia Museum of Art, Philadelphia

OPPOSITE:
The Praying Jew (Rabbi of Vitebsk), 1914
Oil on canvas, 104 x 84 cm (41 x 33 in.)
Kollektion im Obersteg, Basle

37

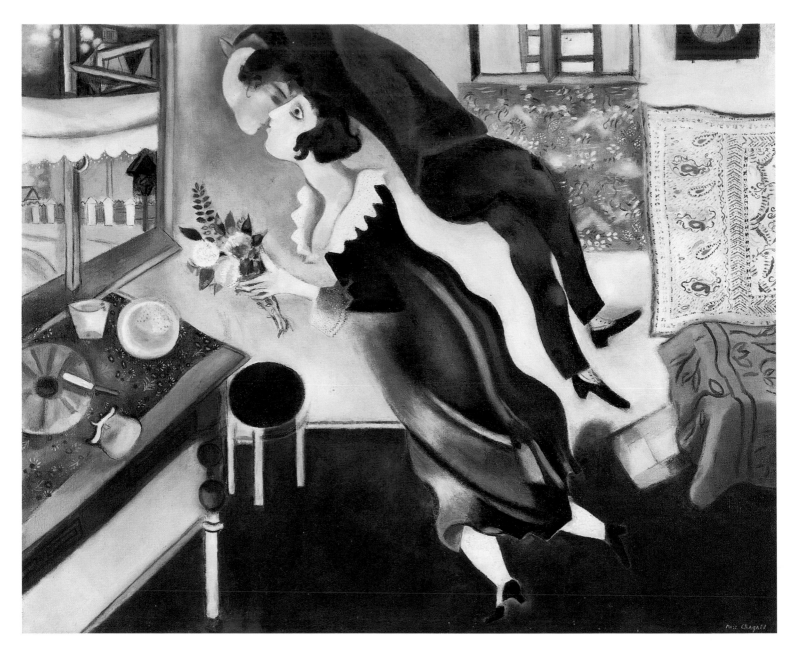

The Birthday, 1915
Oil on canvas, 81 x 100 cm (32 x 39¾ in.)
Museum of Modern Art, acquired through the
Lillie P. Bliss Bequest, New York

OPPOSITE:
Feast Day (Rabbi with Lemon), 1914
Oil on cardboard on canvas,
100 x 81 cm (39½ x 32 in.)
Kunstsammlung Nordrhein-Westfalen,
Düsseldorf

blueness of the sky, love and flowers with her. Dressed all in white or all in black, she has been haunting my paintings, the great central image of my art."

With the energies of a poet, Chagall uses words such as "flow", "haunt" or "hover" to give linguistic expression to the exhilaration and happiness he felt with Bella. The dizzy freedom from gravity we observe in the couple in the painting is, strictly speaking, simply the visual transcript twin of metaphoric language, a faithful reformulation of linguistic ideas into images in paint. The label "poetry" has time and time again been attached to Marc Chagall's art, and in this identification of written and visual language it proves apt.

The painter and his bride dreamt of carefree serenity in the country, and the picturesque idyll – lying back in the grass – became real in a painting: *The Poet Reclining* (p. 40) shows the poet stretched full-length, matching the lower edge of the picture. Overhead, with nothing to decide whether we are seeing the poet's vision or a real scene, we see an idyll of Nature: "Alone at last in the country. Woods, pine trees, solitude. The moon behind the wood. The pig in the sty, and through the window the horse in the fields. The sky a lilac colour," Chagall recalls in *My Life*.

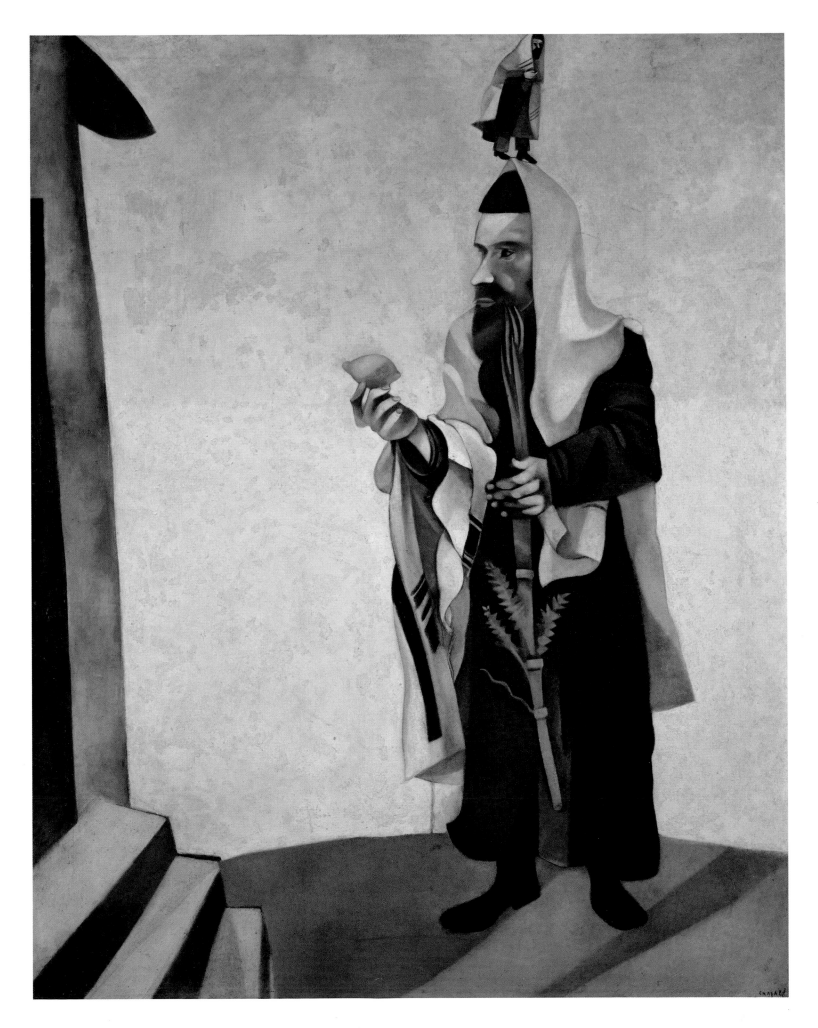

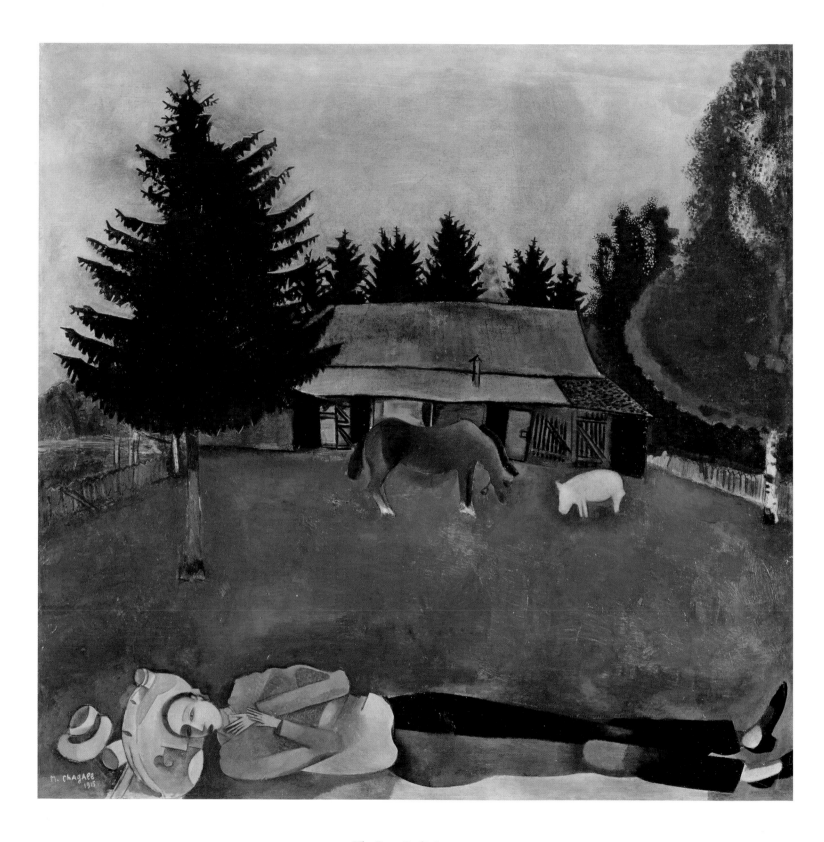

The Poet Reclining, 1915
Oil on cardboard, 77 x 77.5 cm (30¼ x 30½ in.)
Tate, London

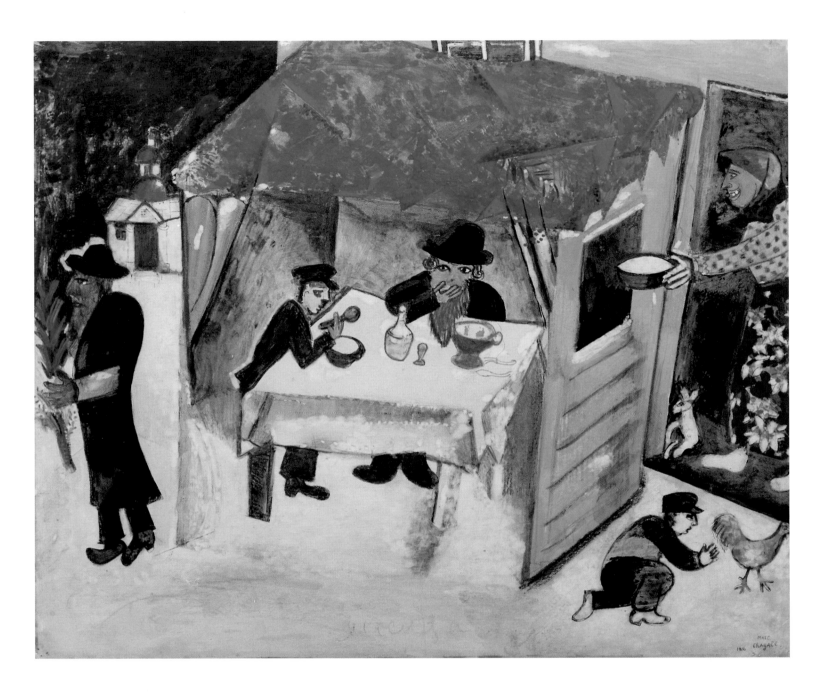

The Feast of the Tabernacles, 1916
Gouache, 33 x 41 cm (13 x 16 in.)
Galerie Rosengart, Lucerne

As in the case of the poet in the painting, the autobiography gives no definite indication whether an actual experience is being described or merely the picture. What gives enduring life to poetry, that highly deliberate game played with ambiguity and lack of clarity, is precisely the blurring of the fictive and the real such as Chagall offers us here; and yet, however much they may toy with poeticism, these paintings are nevertheless conjurations of a world where all is well. They afford ways of escaping the tough reality of the war years.

Soon, though, that reality overtook Chagall. Military service proved unavoidable. To get out of being sent to the front, and thus to certain injury of body and soul, Chagall took work in his brother-in-law's office in the capital, where essential war work was being done, which rated as equivalent to serving at the front. And so Chagall spent his days in St Petersburg, monotonously stamping papers, disinclined to paint.

In Paris, with its own tremendously active art scene, Chagall had learnt little of Russia's remarkable artistic evolution, of the avant-garde's progress from

"Down with Naturalism, Impressionism, and realistic Cubism ... Let us indulge our own lunacy! What is needed is a purifying bloodbath, a revolution in the depths and not on the surface."

MARC CHAGALL

41

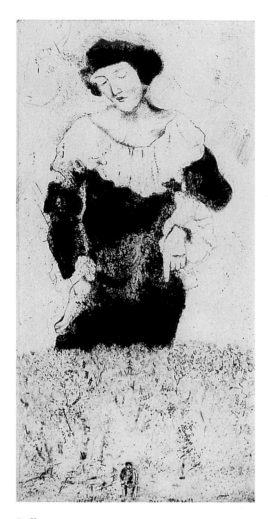

Bella, 1925
Etching and cold needle, 22.5 x 11.6 cm
(8¾ x 4½ in.)

"In the mornings and evenings she would bring
to my studio cakes she had baked with loving
care, fried fish, boiled milk, colourful fabrics,
and even boards of wood to use as an easel. All I
had to do was open my window and in streamed
the blueness of the sky, love and flowers with
her. Dressed all in white or all in black, she has
long been haunting my paintings, the great central image of my art."

MARC CHAGALL, in *My Life*

OPPOSITE:
Bella with White Collar, 1917
Oil on canvas, 149 x 72 cm (58½ x 28¼ in.)
Private collection

regional to international importance. In St Petersburg he was now able to engage
in new developments. In 1912 he had participated in the group show entitled
Donkey's Tail, sending his painting *The Dead Man* from Paris – the aesthetics
of that exhibition were not unlike his own. In 1916 Chagall somewhat belatedly
turned to the Primitivism then being practised by Nathalie Gontcharova and
Michael Larionov, and the effect can be seen particularly clearly in *The Feast
of the Tabernacles* (p. 41). Figures of a deliberate awkwardness move across a
space, angular and as if they had been placed on a background they had not the
slightest connection with. As if seen with a child's perspective, they are reduced
to complete profiles or completely frontal images; there are no intermediate
shades or nuances, since this would not fit the robust simplicity of the scene. It is
only in his rendering of the summer-house roof, with its vague gestures towards
Cubism, that Chagall demonstrates that the crude fashioning of the picture is
deliberate and not due to any lack of skill. Locked away in the cramped and
spartan confines of a war economy office, the artist could not rise to that fleet-
footed choreographic brushwork that distinguishes the paintings inspired by
Bella (see right). The plain and pithy working of *The Feast of the Tabernacles*
reflects Chagall's emotional condition.

An event was to follow which, according to Chagall, was the most important
in his life, and which was to keep the artist, and many more besides, in suspense
for years to come. At the heart of the nation, in the capital, he watched the sig-
nals for struggle against the hopelessly outdated Czarist regime grow into revolution. During the ten days that shook the world, St Petersburg was in the hands
of the Reds.

"Thus saith the Lord God: Behold, O my people, I will open your graves, and
cause you to come up out of your graves, and bring you into the land of Israel."
These words of the vision of Ezekiel are inscribed in Hebrew lettering above
Cemetery Gates (p. 45), which Chagall painted at that very time.

A mood of turbulent change prevailed throughout the nation, and thus
Chagall's use of the Old Testament prophecy for a present rejoicing in its future
by no means seems blasphemous. The Bolsheviks had taken Russia out of the
war, and the Jews at long last had equal citizens' rights with other Russians. The
early days of the Revolution were marked by untroubled optimism.

Lenin appointed Anatoli Lunacharski head of his Ministry of Culture.
Chagall had known Lunacharski in Paris, where the émigré was making his living as a journalist, writing for Russian-language publications. In September 1918,
this acquaintanceship resulted in an official position for Chagall: he was made
Fine Arts Commissar in Vitebsk. Art was highly valued in the opening phase of
the Revolution, and it was hoped that aesthetics and politics would inspire each
other in their strivings for a more human future. Communists saw both art, and
their conception of the state as being opposed to bourgeois attitudes, as being
interdependent, and (by virtue of being progressive and avant-garde) as offering
them the chance of a better world. The old dream of art autonomously practised
for its own sake was to be replaced by an art engaged with reality.

Chagall, full of enthusiasm, plunged headlong into his new position as a pro-
fessional aesthetician; he organized exhibitions, opened museums, and restarted
classes at the Vitebsk Academy of Art. And presently this confirmed individual-
ist and resolute advocate of the strange and unusual was to be found putting the
case for the power of anonymity and equality: "Believe me, the working people,

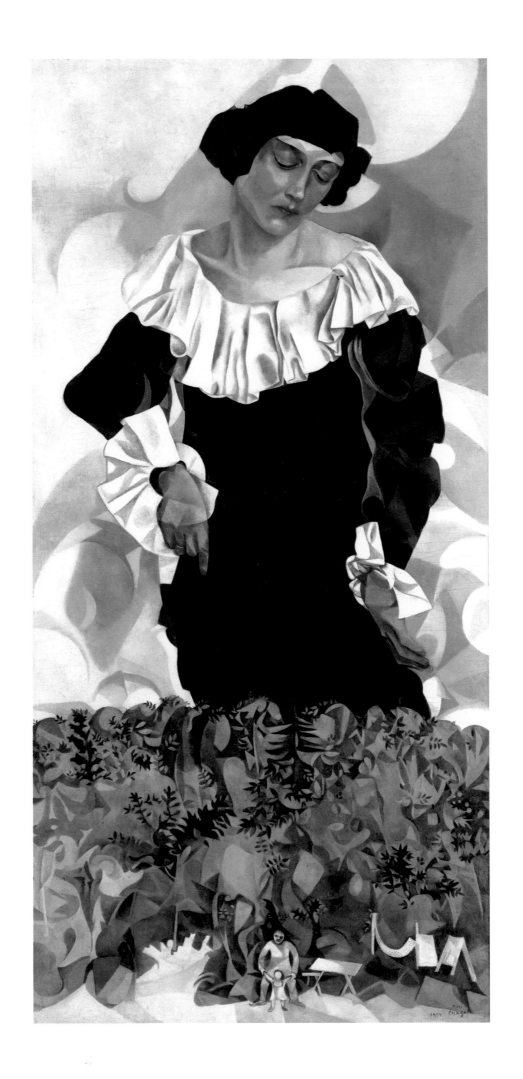

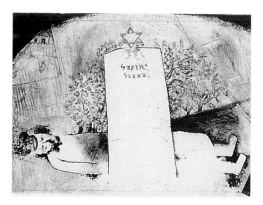

The Artist's Father's Grave, 1922
Leaf 19 in the series *My Life*
Cold needle etching,
10.8 x 14.9 cm (4¼ x 5¾ in.)

"Clad in a Russian smock, a leather briefcase
under my arm, I gave the perfect impression of
a Soviet functionary."
MARC CHAGALL, in *My Life*

OPPOSITE:
Cemetery Gates, 1917
Oil on canvas, 87 x 68.5 cm (34½ x 27 in.)
Private collection

once they have been transformed, will be ready to storm the heights of art and culture." Chagall was quite the Communist, without reservation.

Chagall planned to mark the first anniversary of the Revolution with colourful celebratory decorations all over Vitebsk. Although he largely kept to the decreed ideology in such works as *War on the Palaces*, the reaction of orthodox comrades was unanimous: "Why is the cow green and why is the horse flying in the sky?" they asked, puzzled, according to Chagall. "What has it got to do with Marx and Lenin?"

The painter had scarcely begun to identify with his new cause when he was confronted with bull-headed demands for the political applicability of his art. *The Painter: To the Moon* (p. 47), dated 1917 by Chagall but very likely done no earlier than 1919, is Chagall's response, and stubbornly insists on artistic inspiration. The familiar figure of the painter reflectively lost in his dreams hovers through the picture, removed from this world into a sphere of imaginary and (as it were) heavenly rapture. His head is crowned with laurels; this age-old symbol of a poet's fame is meant as an eloquent testimony to the painter's intention to create realities of his own.

Not least because Vitebsk was largely spared the terrible food shortages that soon ravaged the land, the Academy of Art, under its director Chagall, soon had an impressive list of famous teachers on its staff. One by one, the *crème* of the Russian avant-garde moved to the provinces, and illustrious names such as El Lissitzky and Kasimir Malevich brought an air of bohemianism to Vitebsk. Soon, conflicts over the direction of true art had begun to jeopardize Chagall's future.

In 1915 Malevich had caused a sensation with his *Black Square on a White Ground*, and had become established internationally as one of the leaders of the new art. The cerebral equilibrium of abstract zones of colour that Malevich advocated in the name of "pure painting", and his thesis that art should abandon all links with given reality, were thorns in Chagall's flesh. While Chagall was away on a trip to Moscow he was deposed by a palace revolution, and the free academy was declared a Suprematist institute. True, Chagall was restored to both his office and his esteem on his return; but he had conceived a deep distrust of the Revolution and its notion of art. In May 1920 Chagall left Vitebsk, and moved with his family to Moscow.

Still, even he had not kept totally free of Malevich's influence. *Peasant Life* (p. 46), dated 1917 but in fact done in 1919 in Vitebsk, clearly evidences a link with Malevich's programme with its meditative balance of monochrome geometrical shapes. But Chagall has peopled this abstract grid with his usual personnel and re-interpreted the colour fields in terms of areas of real life; the man with the whip and the woman with the animal occupy these zones in archetypal confrontation. This peaceful geometrical order, which served Malevich as a metaphor for the inner world of thought and feeling, is transformed by Chagall into a concrete basic idea, a core repertoire of motifs for the execution of genre scenes.

The family led their life in the new capital in considerable poverty. Chagall was fond of the stage, and created designs for Moscow's Jewish Theatre, but he earned only enough for the bare essentials. He made monumental murals for the foyer and auditorium, with allegorical images of aspects of theatre; *Green Violinist* (p. 49), painted in 1923–4, is a replica of the mural depicting music, and a faithful reduced-size version of an original in the Moscow theatre. The familiar

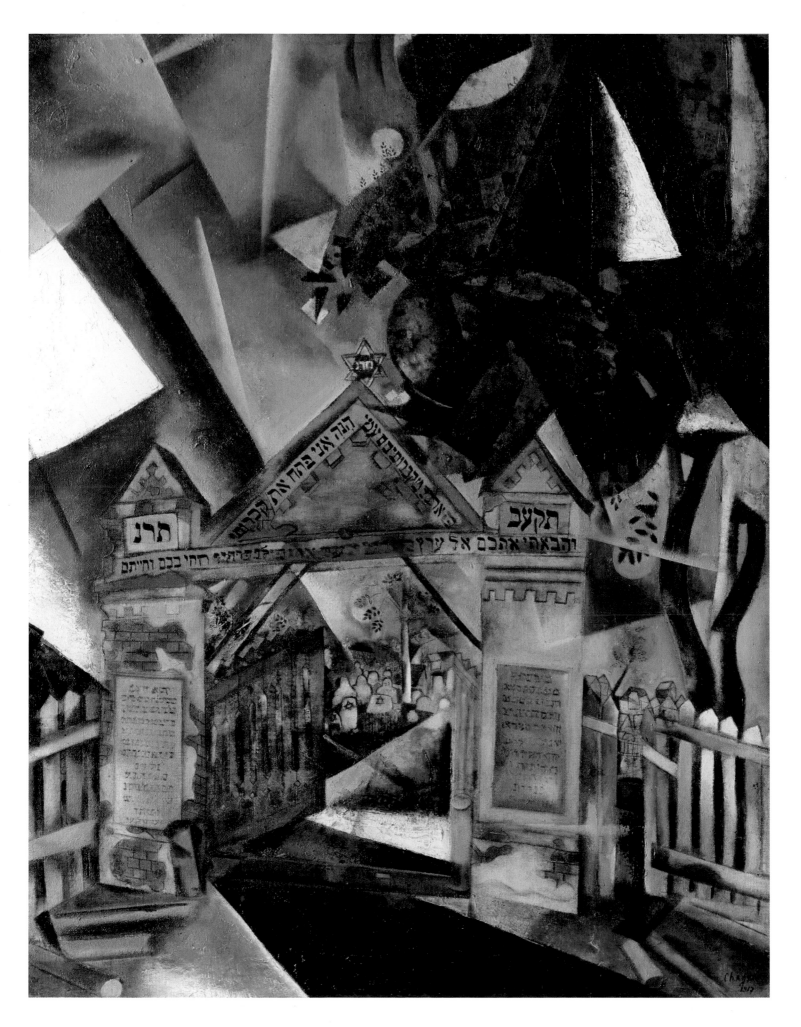

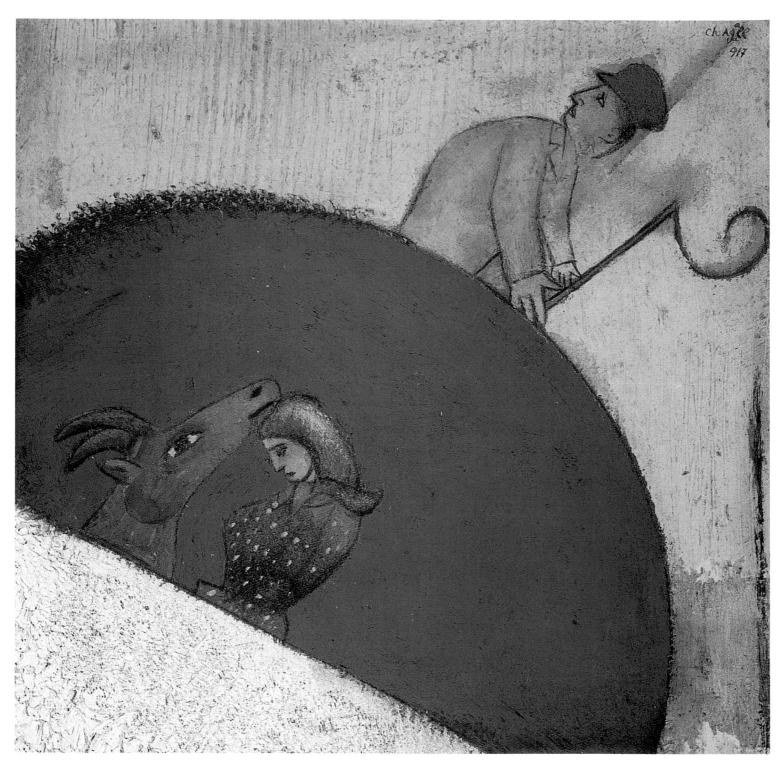

Peasant Life (The Stable; Night; Man with Whip), 1917
Oil on cardboard, 21 x 21.5 cm (8¼ x 8½ in.)
Solomon R. Guggenheim Museum, New York

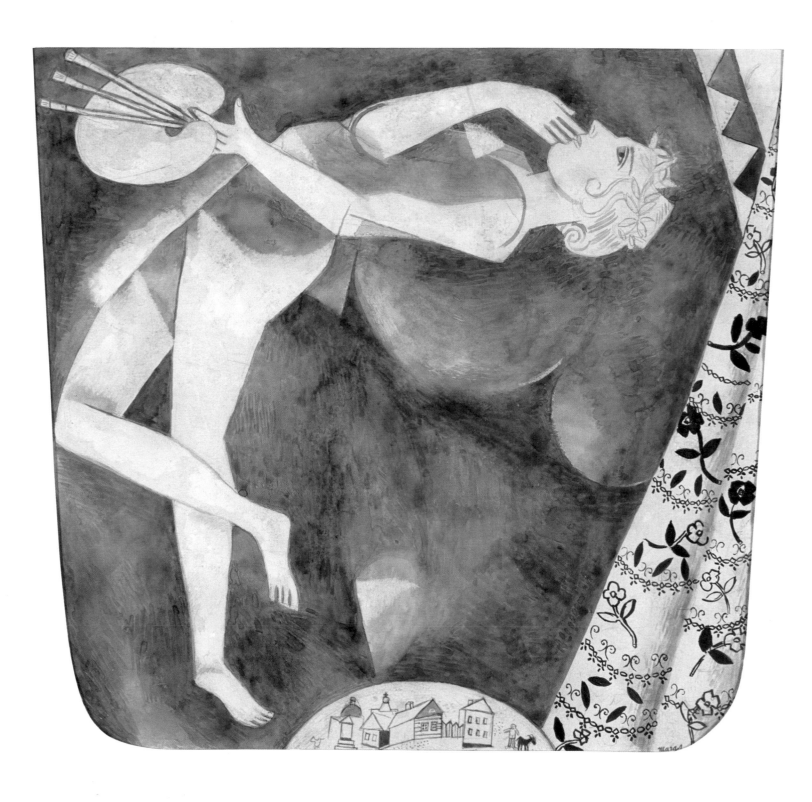

The Painter: To the Moon, 1917
Gouache and watercolour on paper, 32 x 30 cm (12½ x 11¾ in.)
Marcus Diener Collection, Basle

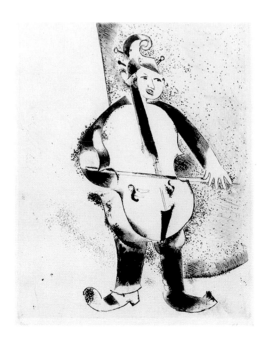

The Musician, 1922
Additional leaf in the series *My Life*
Cold needle etching,
27.5 x 21.6 cm (10¾ x 8½ in.)

figure of the fiddler has lost none of its suggestive power for Chagall, and the image conjures forth another world at a time of deep depression.

The support the state gave artists was scaled according to the political usefulness of their works. Chagall was placed very far down in the grant hierarchy, since none other than Malevich was responsible for classifying artists, and Malevich had a low opinion of his fellow artist.

"I think the Revolution could be a great thing if it retained its respect for what is other and different," wrote Chagall in *My Life*, which he was completing at the time.

It was this respect, a respect for his own affection for the unusual, that he felt a lack of in the new order; the totalitarian tendency to steamroll everything level had left his appeals to the power of fantasy unheeded. With no money, success or prospects, Chagall no longer had any reason to stay in the nation that was now known as the Soviet Union. Lunacharski got the family a passport so that they could leave.

Chagall now recollected Herwarth Walden, the Berlin gallery owner, and the success he had been denied for so many years. He planned to pick up the threads of his career in Berlin and re-establish a secure financial footing for his future by selling paintings there; when he arrived in the city in summer 1922, it turned out that his name did indeed have some currency. Walden had sold the pictures Chagall had left in Berlin and had paid the money into an account for the artist. However, high inflation had now hit Germany and the money had become valueless, so that Chagall found himself with neither pictures nor funds. He went to court over the matter, and a few of the paintings, hastily bought back, were restored to him by way of compensation. But he literally had to start all over again.

OPPOSITE:
The Green Violinist, 1923–4
Oil on canvas, 198 x 108.6 cm (78 x 42¾ in.)
Solomon R. Guggenheim Museum, New York

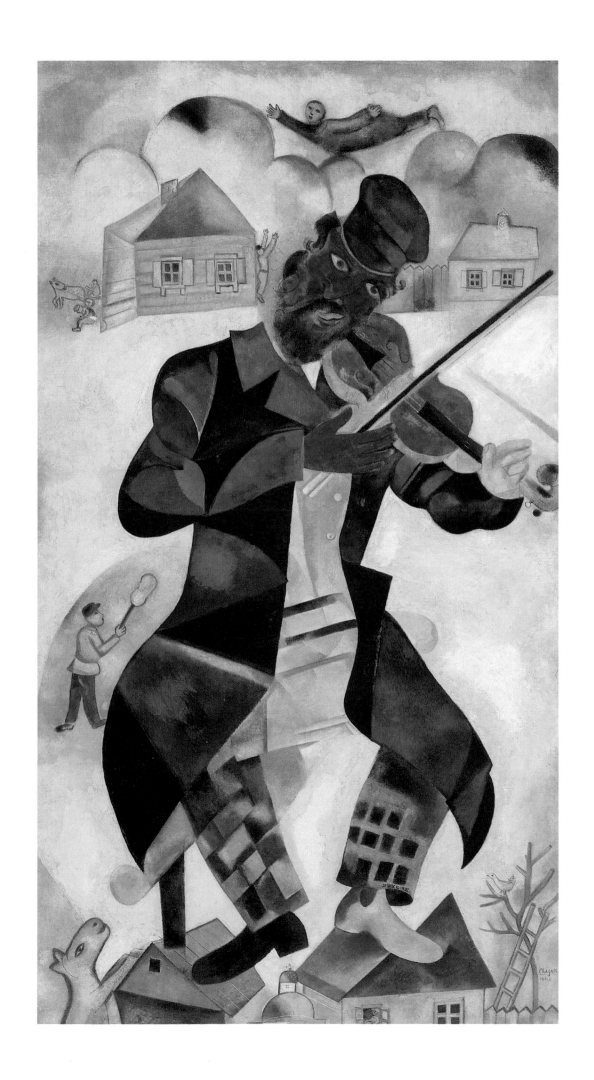

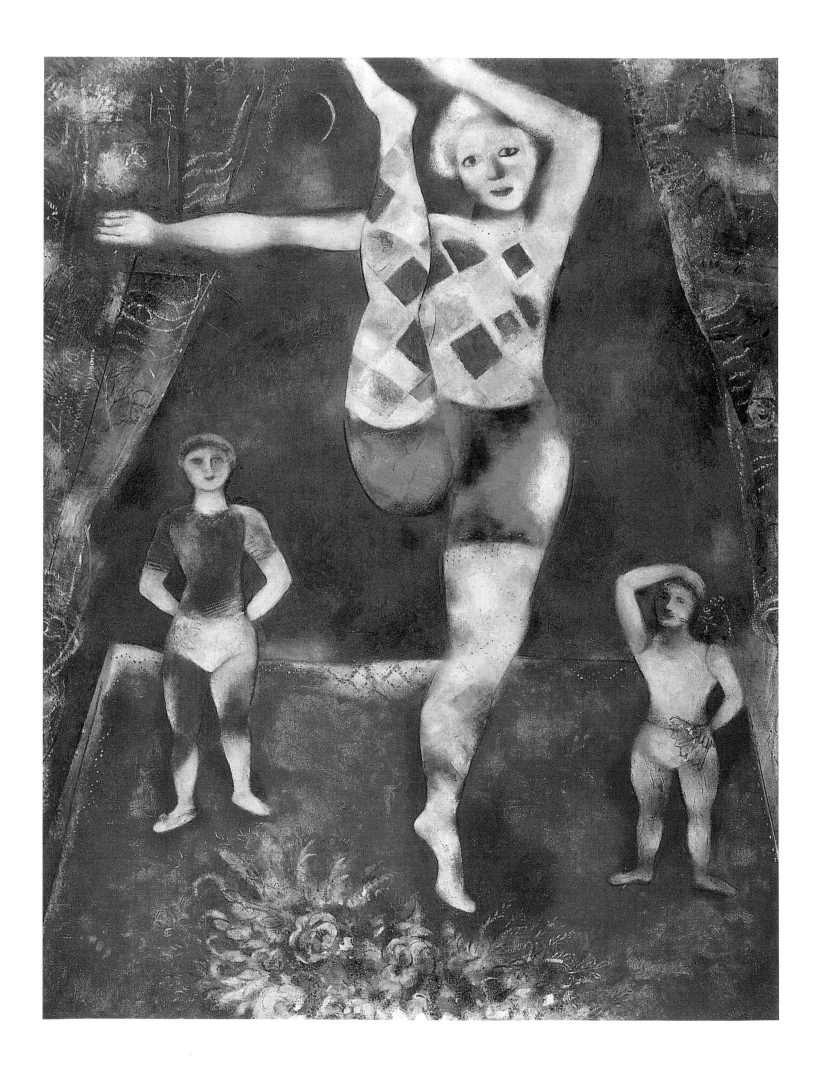

France and America
1923–1948

Chagall's memoirs in *My Life*, finished in 1922, make best sense read with the upheaval and removal from Moscow to Paris in mind. Not yet forty, the artist took an autobiographical, retrospective look at a past that had been far from uneventful, and tried to draw up a balance sheet on his own life. The gentle irony that turns the autonomous world of his paintings into the diary-like impressions of childhood is also to be found in these recollections. His art was lost in the gutters of the market, but his recollections were still all there.

The book was meant to be published by Paul Cassirer in Berlin and was also intended to serve as a sign of life for his old friends in France. But for the time being, only a portfolio of twenty etchings (Chagall's illustrations to the text) was produced; the book edition was not published until 1931 in Paris, Bella having translated it from Russian into French. Still, the great Parisian dealer Ambroise Vollard, mentor of the Cubists and a friendly father-figure to Picasso in particular, commissioned Chagall to illustrate Nikolai Gogol's *Dead Souls*, and on 1 September 1923, Chagall left for Paris and a new artistic career.

"What I first set eyes on was a trough. Simple, massive, semi-hollow, semi-oval. A junkshop trough. Once I got in, I filled it completely." These are the opening words of *My Life*. *The Watering Trough* (p. 52) recalls the memoirs' opening and emblematically emphasizes Chagall's continuing ties to the past times from which he could not break loose.

Perhaps working on the book by his fellow countryman, Gogol, revived his recollections of Russia; at any rate, as his fame increased, this kind of subject-matter came to be his trademark, with Chagall not so much focusing attention on the world of the *shtetl* as quoting himself. The woman and the pig are both bending over the trough in unison. They have the same long backs, and their heads are in the same profile position – they both need water: tongue-in-cheek, the artist is pointing out the affinity of human and animal. The scene has its own unity, and in its absurdity has the flavour of the earlier genre scenes observed from further away; the fine, subtle colouring, with its unmistakably French character, contributes to this unity. There are two versions of this painting, their colour schemes quite distinct. A typically Western feeling for the emotive qualities of colouring is superimposed atmospherically on to the earthy subject-matter drawn from Chagall's homeland. It was a strategy Chagall was to perfect in the years ahead.

In the early phase of this new Paris period, Chagall was especially fond of making two versions of a painting, as if by creating it in duplicate he could guarantee his own existence against the predatory machinations of the market.

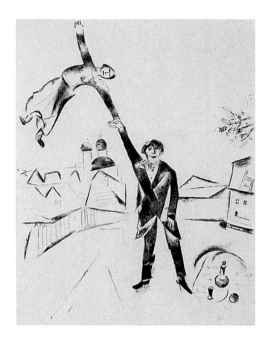

The Walk, 1922
Additional leaf in the series *My Life*
Cold needle etching, 25 x 19 cm (9¾ x 7½ in.)

OPPOSITE:
The Three Acrobats, 1926
Oil on canvas, 117 x 89 cm (46 x 35 in)
Private collection

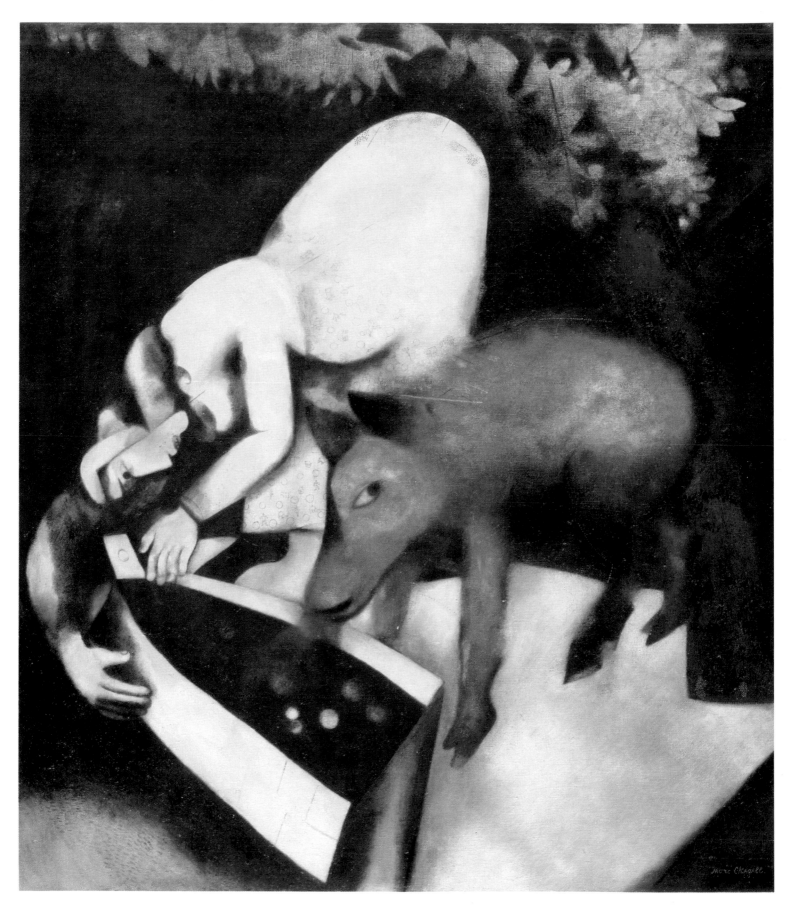

The Watering Trough, 1925
Oil on canvas, 99.5 x 88.5 cm (39¼ x 34¾ in.)
Philadelphia Museum of Art, Philadelphia

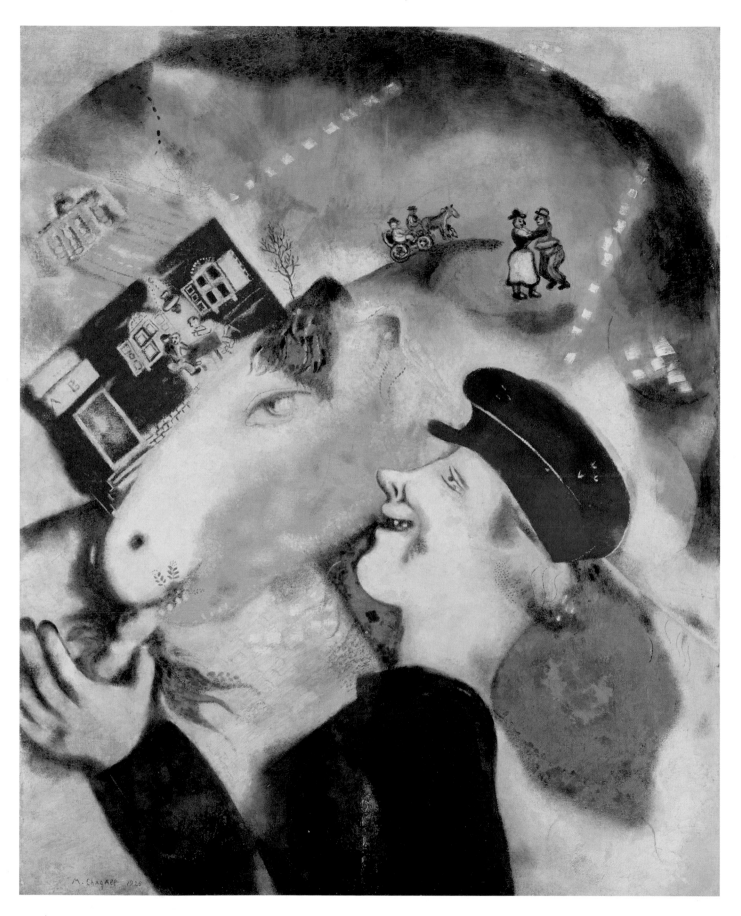

Peasant Life, 1925
Oil on canvas, 101 x 80 cm (39¾ x 31½ in.)
Albright-Knox Art Gallery, Buffalo (N.Y.)

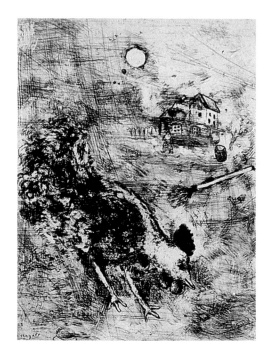

The Cock and the Pearl, *c.* 1927–30
Table 11 in the illustrations for the *Fables of La Fontaine* (published 1952)
Etching, 30.2 x 22.8 cm (12 x 9 in.)

OPPOSITE:
The Rooster, 1929
Oil on canvas, 81 x 65 cm (32 x 25½ in.)
Madrid, Museo Thyssen-Bomemisza

He also set about re-doing some of the paintings that had gone missing, using reproductions or working from memory. What prompted him to these repetitive labours may have been not only the wish to repair the ravages of war and make good the loss to his art, but also a sense that, with the paintings, a part of himself had been lost.

This is by no means an inflated stylization of himself. Rather, it reflects a profound faith in the power of images, a faith that had led the Jews to veto image-making, particularly religious ones. A veto and a cult are two sides of the same coin: Chagall the Jew proves in this to be deeply rooted in his people's traditions. The ancient magic power of pictures, which Chagall liked to describe with the untranslatable word "*chimie*", lives on in the artist's refusal to make saleable objects of his works. He could adapt to his audience's wishes and needs in a way most of his fellow artists were unable to do, but it was an adaptability that respected the autonomous authority of the finished painting.

The subject-matter of *I and the Village* (p. 21), one of the paintings of which Chagall made a second copy, reappears in the 1925 work *Peasant Life* (p. 53). Once again we see archetypal figures that personify a quality of simplicity in a visionary setting: human and animal figures, along with a sense of idyllic security, constitute the genre's *sine qua non*. However, the geometrical grid that made the juxtapositions in the earlier painting possible has now been replaced, in compositional terms, by a principle of free association. The man feeding the horse, whose profile is the base of the house, now has a complementary rather than contrastive effect.

What inspired this painting was not so much rustic life in Russia (which Chagall, after the things he had experienced during the Revolution, was less prepared to glamorize), as an image Chagall had of himself. The atmospheric content of the colour scheme, along with the relaxation of the strict grid, are a commentary on his early period viewed from the vantage-point of the latest aesthetic trends. Surrealism had replaced Cubism, and Chagall felt an affinity through the liberation from self-imposed patterns of order and the reckless espousal of the kind of disorder that is typical of dreams.

"Chagall, and only Chagall, provided painting with the triumphant advent of metaphor." Thus wrote André Breton, singing Chagall's praises, and eulogizing his poetic qualities, as late as 1945. Nevertheless, Chagall's relationship to the Surrealists was torn, whatever their theoretician-in-chief might say. Long before them, impelled by the elemental power of his home-land's folk art, he had discovered the significance of dreams, visions and the non-rational for his own work. The Surrealists, whose antirational approach to art drew upon similar sources, repeatedly tried to win Chagall over, but Chagall saw their homage to the power of the unconscious as a way of pandering to the currents of taste and a wilful parade of illogicality, and was unable to identify with them. His artistic credo came straight from the heart: "The entire world within us is reality, perhaps more real than the visible world. If one calls everything that seems illogical fantasy or a fairy-tale, all one proves is that one has not understood Nature." To be attached to one's dreams and yet to advocate reality constituted no contradiction in Chagall's eyes.

The family lived in the Avenue d'Orléans, in the apartment where Lenin had stayed before them. The rooms, crammed with the magic of oriental decor,

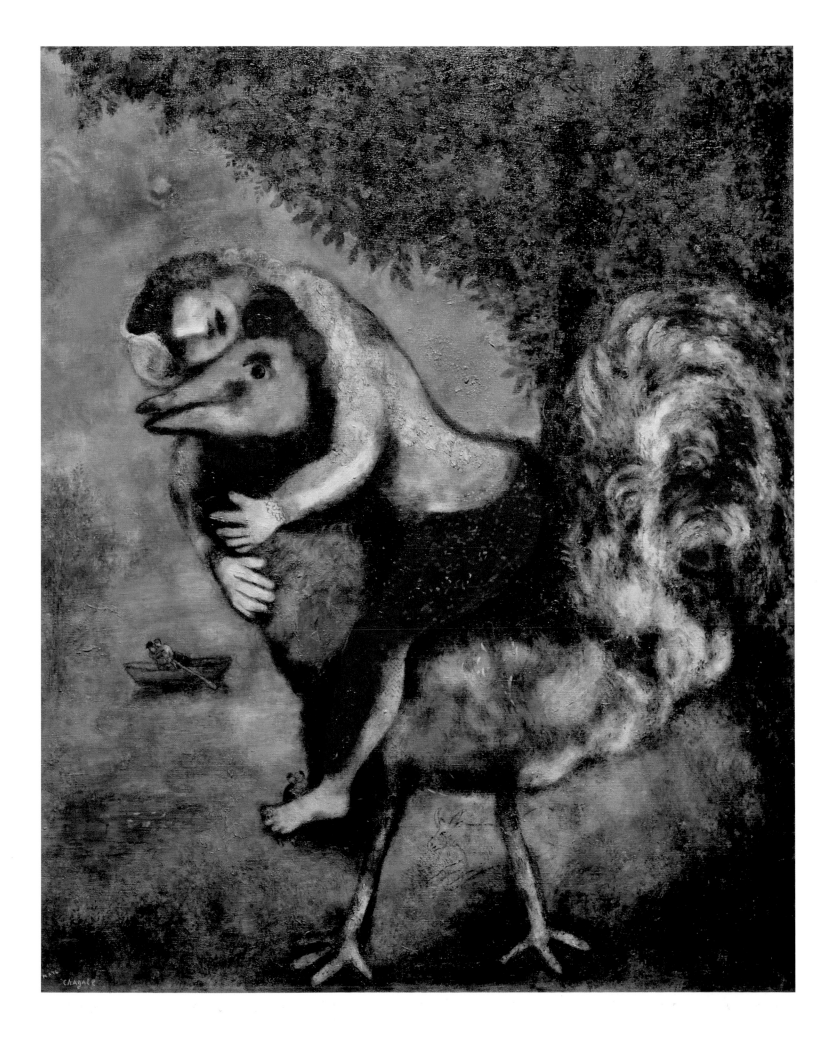

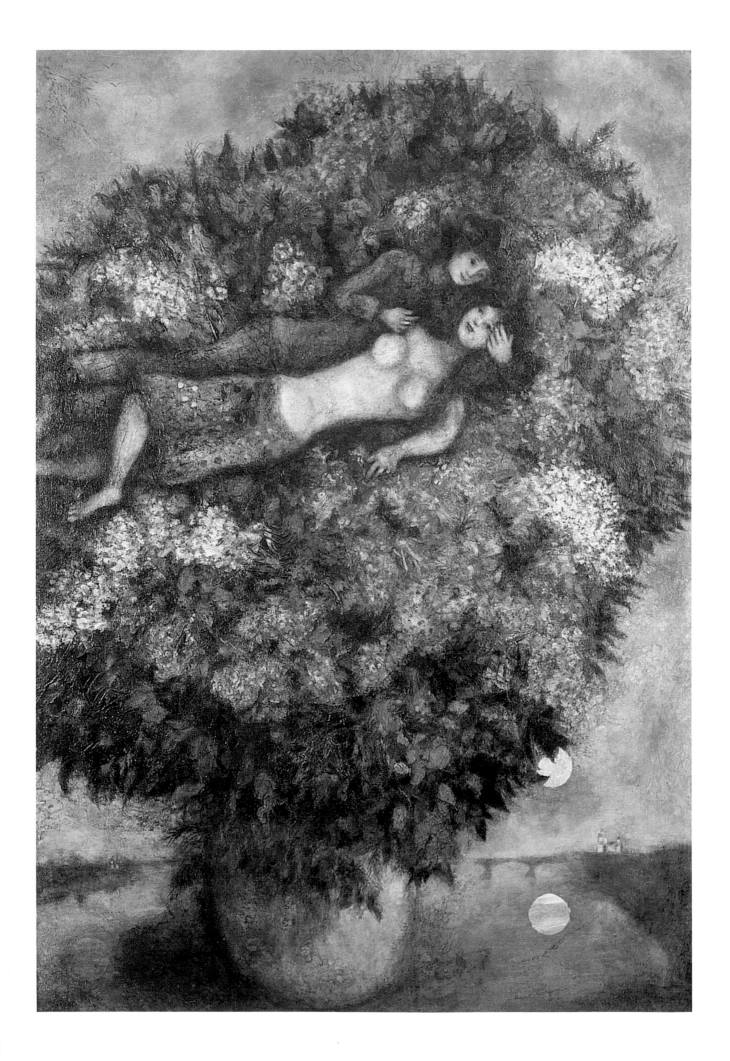

were an oasis of the exotic in the cool atmosphere of the big city. They were dominated by carpets and cushions, and the ambience matched Chagall's public image: the aura of the unfamiliar and mysterious that his pictorial images evoked increasingly extended to the artist himself, and became a means of self-publicizing that came to accompany him on every step throughout his long career.

In 1924 the first Chagall retrospective was seen in Paris, and in 1926 he had his first New York exhibition. From the mid-1920s, at the latest, the provincial Russian's visions had become public property; and both in his lifestyle and in his work, subtle changes in the direction of his wider audience's taste began to become apparent.

In *The Three Acrobats* (p. 50), the central figure leaps forward, with a final athletic motion, to receive applause and bouquets at the edge of the stage. Chagall had always loved the world of the circus and had been enthralled by its blend of dance, theatre, music and language. This painting (done in 1926) is the earliest of Chagall's works with the circus as subject. It took him a relatively long time to express in paint a subject he had long been inclined towards. An explanation may lie in the pressure he was now under: to adapt.

For the first time he now seemed willing to apply his visionary visual terms to a realm of experience where such a quality was natural and, in any case, characteristic. The magic of the motif and that of the artistic strategy now met, and threatened to cancel each other out. Where Picasso had mercilessly confronted his tumblers and harlequins with reality, Chagall's pictures of acrobats have problems with tautology.

Not only the subject but also the clarity and near-classical coolness of the presentation remind us of Picasso's work. The framing of the central figure by the smaller flanking ones, the echoing of this triangular composition by the canopy-like curtain, the robust physicality of the figures (with an effect like statues), create an almost academic repose that reflects a centuries-old code of beauty. The figurative emphasis is now on artistic virtuosity as assessed by the touchstone of pictorial tradition; the chaos of visions clamouring for expression has been ousted in favour of the timeless norm of classic simplicity. The painting has all the atmosphere characteristic of Chagall's work, but also a highly elaborate, even overdone touch of the Old Masters.

In his biography of Chagall, Franz Meyer quotes an aphorism that sums up the two artists: "Picasso stood for the triumph of the intellect, Chagall for the glory of the heart." The two now established a relaxed friendship.

To Marc Chagall:

"Ass or cow rooster or horse
Through to the body of a fiddle
Singing man a single bird
Nimbly dancing with his wife
A couple immersed in spring
Gold of the grass lead of the sky
Marked off by blue flames
By the freshness of the dew
The blood shimmers the heart beats
A couple the first reflection
And in a vaulted dome of snow
The full vine sketches in
A face with lips of moonlight
That never sleeps at night."

PAUL ELUARD

OPPOSITE:
Lovers in the Lilacs, 1930
Oil on canvas, 128 x 87 cm (50½ x 34¼ in.)
Private collection

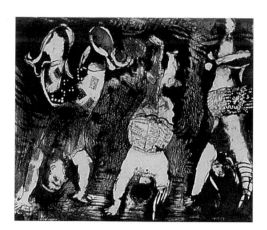

Three Acrobats, 1926
Etching and aquatint,
34.2 x 37.3 cm (13½ x 14¾ in.)

The dreamy elegance of the loving couple in *The Rooster* (p. 55), where the monumental bird has replaced the lover, belongs in that twilit world that can be grasped only in terms of mood and emotion. The bliss these two are enjoying is shared by two other couples, who are secluded in the background of the painting and in the security of their affections.

The love poetry written by Chagall in such works, and the tender elation, peaks in *Lovers in the Lilacs* (p. 56), painted in 1930. The couple, idyllically bedded down in a giant bouquet, are wholly immersed in the timelessness of love. Following an ages-old pictorial code, Chagall has here incorporated two of his central motifs: an icon showing the Madonna Platytera was his inspiration, a representation of the pregnant Virgin Mary with the Child painted on her belly for clarity's sake. In painting the mare with the foal in her womb (cf. *The Cattle Dealer*, p. 31), Chagall had already echoed this treatment; now he abstracted it into an explanation of the symbolic dimension that was always in his motifs. Without doubt, this approach simplified the business of decoding his pictorial messages, and helped Chagall to the popularity his work enjoyed at the time, but at the same time the wish to be comprehensible lent the paintings a touch of romanticism that seemed somewhat outmoded.

Yet, that first decade in Paris, as the artist tells us, was "the happiest time of my life". A contract with the art-dealer Bemheim removed his financial worries, the family was able to move into a villa, and soon they were taking their summer holidays in the south of France for granted. This more lavish way of life, this private happiness, was accompanied by a compulsive turn to the opulent in Chagall's work: the carefree naïvety of the pictures reflects the painter's own untroubled existence, and the magical atmosphere replaces that liveliness of subject-matter that requires an eventful reality as a corrective.

His mood, however, was shortly to darken. In a 1933 painting entitled *Solitude* (p. 60), the merry dance of loving couples is ousted by profound melancholy. Lost in contemplation, cloaked in his *tallith*, a full-bearded Jew of indeterminate age is sitting in the grass, the scrolls of the Torah unopened in his left hand: the religious tradition of his forefathers affords no balm for his misery, it seems. The sad-eyed cow lying beside him recalls the words of the prophet Hosea: "For Israel slideth back as a back-sliding heifer." (Hosea 4:16.) These figures symbolize the people of the Jewish diaspora, Chagall's people (as the Russian surroundings imply). The picturesque old man can be seen as Ahasverus, the eternal Wandering Jew, roaming the world in uncertainty as to his future. On the horizon, beyond a countryside that is on the whole seen with tender affection, storm clouds are gathering, and their blackness is threatening the angel in the sky.

In 1931 Chagall had visited Palestine, the Promised Land, but in his pictures the result of his travels appears as anything but optimism. Alert to the world he lived in, Chagall recorded notes of discord and unease: the year that saw the barbaric ideology of National Socialism triumphant in Germany also saw repose driven out of Chagall's paintings by a real world of harsh power.

In *Solitude*, Chagall was still using motifs that were very much his own, to indicate dangers that were menacing himself, his people, and all of Europe. It was not the narrative content of the painting, but its atmosphere that conveyed his newly gloomy view of the world; in this respect, it resembled the mood paintings of the 1920s. Another journey, to Poland in the spring of 1935,

OPPOSITE:
The Acrobat, 1930
Oil on canvas, 65 x 32 cm (25½ x 12½ in.)
Musée national d'art moderne, Centre Georges Pompidou, Paris

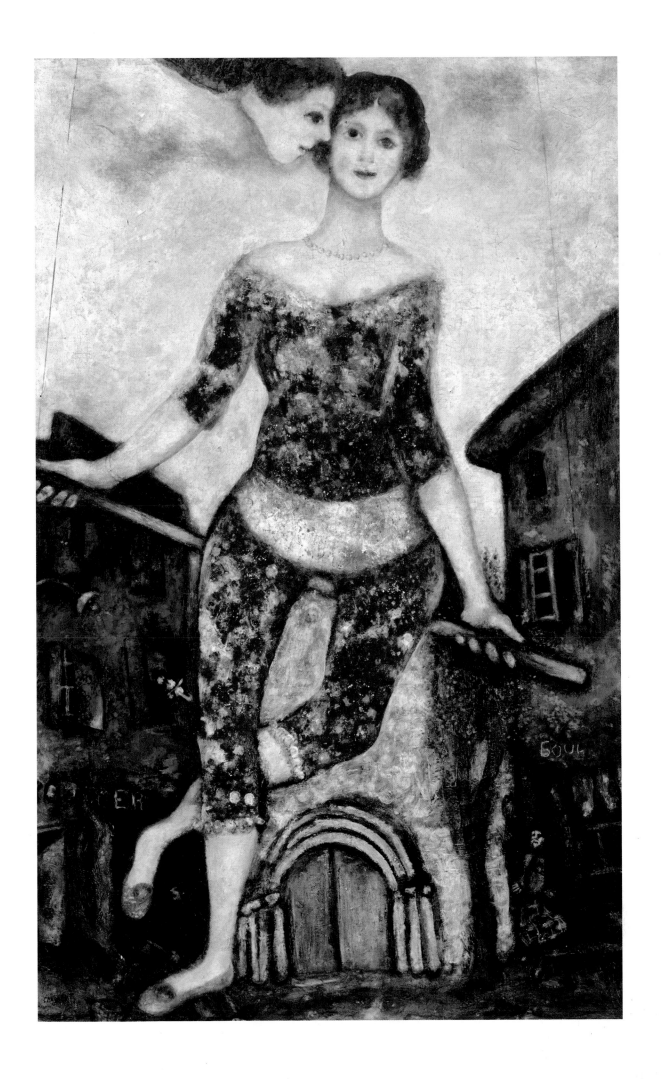

finally convinced Chagall that a new political reality had come to the fore, which his own world of images could no longer ignore: he was deeply affected by what he saw in the Warsaw ghetto, and was present when his friend Dubnow was called a "dirty Jew" in the street. The world of the Jews was no longer a dreamy, cosy sanctum of timeless contentment, but was instead being perverted into a scene of rabid pogroms and racist obsession. And the presence of this existential threat restored a new power of authenticity to Chagall's work.

Fascist assaults on the very core of human morality had been answered by Picasso in what ranks as the finest product of committed historical art in the twentieth century. His *Guernica* (Museo del Prado, Madrid) expressed the full depth of protest that civilization was compelled to make when confronted with political cynicism, and in 1937 the painting was (sadly enough) a major attraction at the World Exhibition in Paris. That same year, Chagall documented his own commitment in *The Revolution* (right), an elegiac work to match the Spanish artist's direct accusation. Chagall's painting is not a response to a specific event, but an attempt to articulate political disquiet and unease in his own terms. Two ways of grasping or shaping the world are juxtaposed in antithesis. To the left, revolutionaries are seen rushing the barricades, their red flags proudly proclaiming the victory of Communism. To the right, this image of unity, standing for political demands for equality, is counterbalanced by the free

Solitude, 1933–4
Oil on canvas, 96 x 158 cm (37¾ x 62¼ in.)
Tel Aviv Museum of Art, Tel Aviv

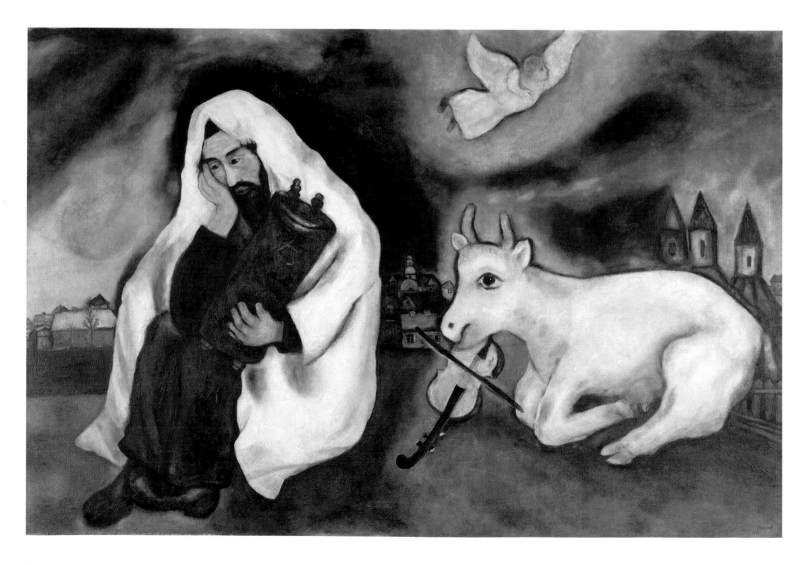

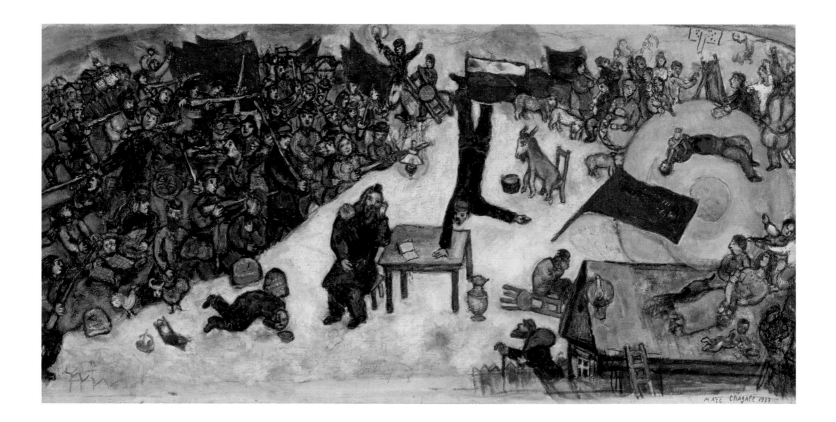

play of the human imagination. We see musicians, clowns and animals playing, the customary loving couple are lolling on the roof of a wooden hut, and in typical Chagall style, the force of gravity has been suspended so that the ubiquitous energies may develop freely. The figure of Lenin links the two zones: balanced acrobatically on one hand, he is showing the revolutionaries the true way to a world of individuality on the other.

"I think the Revolution could be a great thing if it retained its respect for what is other and different," Chagall had written, summing up his Russian experiences in the light of his view of himself as artist. The creative power of the individual is perceived to be the driving-force in the struggle for political liberty. But the old Jew "in solitude" still stirs his thinking about his own future and that of his people...

The painting is vehemently programmatic, and overloaded with significance, so that its capacity for atmosphere and mood has been lost. Its ambitious attempt to find a general, supra-individual relevance and its unsatisfying treatment of the technical problems remind us of Chagall's zeal in his early works: the juxtaposition of archetypes, of symbolically laden shorthand images of the world, is not equal to the task of rendering the complexity of events. Nor was Chagall himself ever satisfied with this answer to Picasso's great masterpiece. In 1943 he was to redo the large-format version of *The Revolution* in three panels, blending the political and religious symbolism in the form of a triptych. The smaller version reproduced here was preserved to testify to the artist's direct involvement with world events (quite distinct from the wish to create timeless works of art).

The second programmatic painting of this period, *White Crucifixion* (p. 63), was done in 1938 and solves the problem better. In 1933, Chagall had described his aesthetic aims in these words: "If a painter is a Jew and paints life, how is he to keep Jewish elements out of his work! But if he is a good

The Revolution, 1937
Oil on canvas, 49.7 x 100.2 cm (19½ x 39½ in.)
Musée national d'art moderne, Centre Georges Pompidou, Paris

"I came to Palestine to examine certain ideas, and I came without a camera, without even a brush. No documentation, no tourist impressions, and nevertheless I am glad to have been there. From far and wide they pour towards the Wailing Wall, bearded Jews in yellow, blue and red robes and with fur caps. Nowhere else do you see so much despair and so much joy; nowhere else are you so shaken and yet so happy as at the sight of this thousand-year-old heap of stones and dust in Jerusalem, in Sefad, in the hills where prophets upon prophets lie buried."

MARC CHAGALL

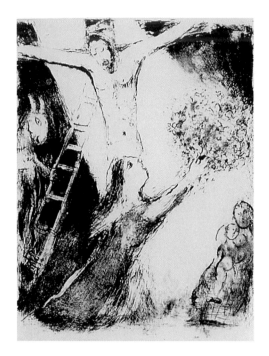

The Crucifixion, 1951–2
Lithograph, 42.3 x 33.5 cm (16½ x 13¼ in.)

painter, his painting will contain a great deal more. The Jewish content will be there, of course, but his art will aim at universal relevance." In the figure of Christ on the Cross, symbolizing the Passion of the Prophet of the Jews and the death of the Christian God who took on the form of a man, Chagall located a universal emblem for the sufferings of this time. Like the "Arma Christi", or the tools and implements shown in traditional Crucifixion scenes, images of confusion are grouped about the Cross. Revolutionary hordes with red flags rampage through a village, looting and burning houses. Refugees in a boat shout for help and gesticulate wildly. A man in Nazi uniform is desecrating a synagogue. Distressed figures in the foreground are trying to escape. Ahasverus, the Wandering Jew, is passing by in silence, stepping over a burning Torah scroll. Old Testament figures are seen hovering, lamenting against the background of desolate darkness. Still, a bright beam of light breaks in from on high, illuminating the white and unblemished figure on the Cross. All trace of his suffering is gone, and worship of his centuries-old authority is seen as a path of hope amid the traumatic events of the present day. Belief in him, so Chagall says, can move the mountains of despair.

Even the gentlest of irony has been eliminated from this picture. Naked existential fear is seen appealing pathetically to the saving power of religion in a way that is unique in Chagall's work. In this painting, and perhaps nowhere else, Chagall's recourse to the traditional repertoire of tricks is quite free of wilful cleverness, and in its very use of scenes of the times, the picture becomes an integrated whole and achieves the timeless depth of an icon. "It is not right to paint pictures with symbols. If a work of art has total authenticity, symbolic meaning will be contained in it of its own accord," Chagall once said. His counterpart to *Guernica* is the devotional painting *White Crucifixion*, which feels its way into that same suffering.

If Chagall had been so sensitively alert to coming horror even before the outbreak of war, once war was declared his feelings became panic-stricken. To be an inner-émigré, and flee the demands of political reality by withdrawing into a confined inner realm of art (as Picasso did in Paris, for example), would have meant idly waiting for the death camps. So it was that in spring 1940 he and his family moved to Gordes, in Provence, where the sheer distance from Nazi Germany guaranteed them a certain safety.

In Gordes, Chagall completed *The Three Candles* (p. 64) in 1940, after having worked at it for two years. Isolated from cultural life and in constant fear of internment, he reviewed his repertoire of images in a quite manic manner: the artiste, the loving couple and the village, mutely available to the painter, consolidate his safety from danger. Melancholy colours predominate, and the fearfulness expressed in the timid gestures of the figures acquires a still-life rigidity, like an emblem of transience, and is transfigured by the symbolism of dying candles into a sombre memento mori.

The French government came to an agreement with the Nazis, and France could no longer be considered safe for Chagall. He was even seized during a raid in Marseilles and threatened with being handed over to the Germans, but American intervention rescued him. While vast numbers of his people were setting off on the tragic journey to destruction, the famous painter was able to fall back upon public help. On 7 May, Chagall and his family embarked for the United States. The myth of the Wandering Jew, of Jewry restlessly on

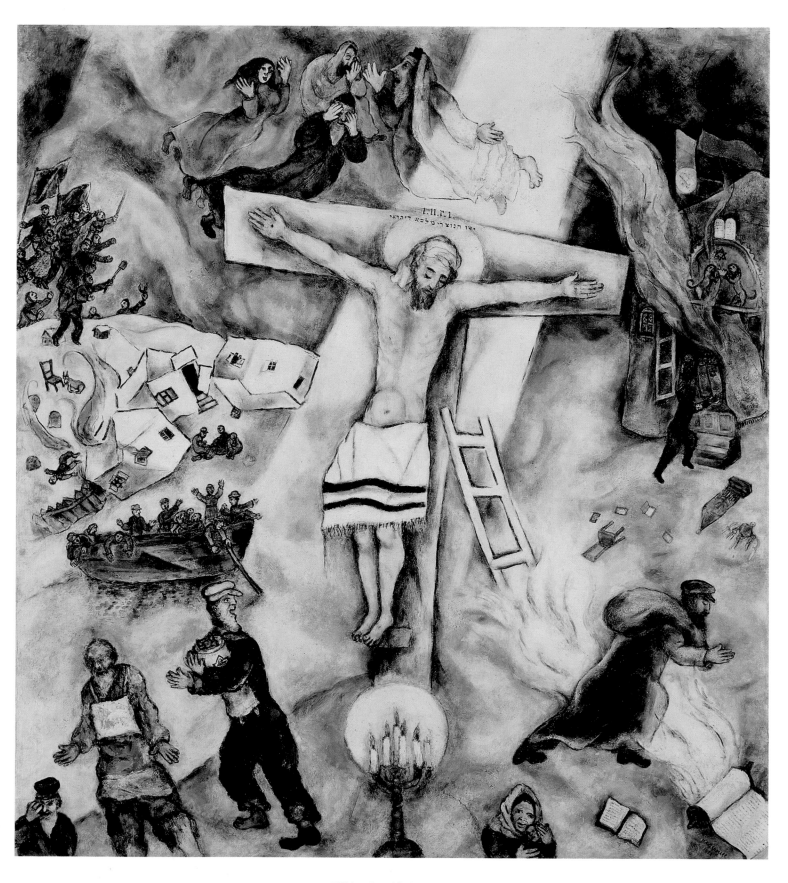

White Crucifixion, 1938
Oil on canvas, 155 x 140 cm (61 x 55 in.)
Art Institute of Chicago, Chicago

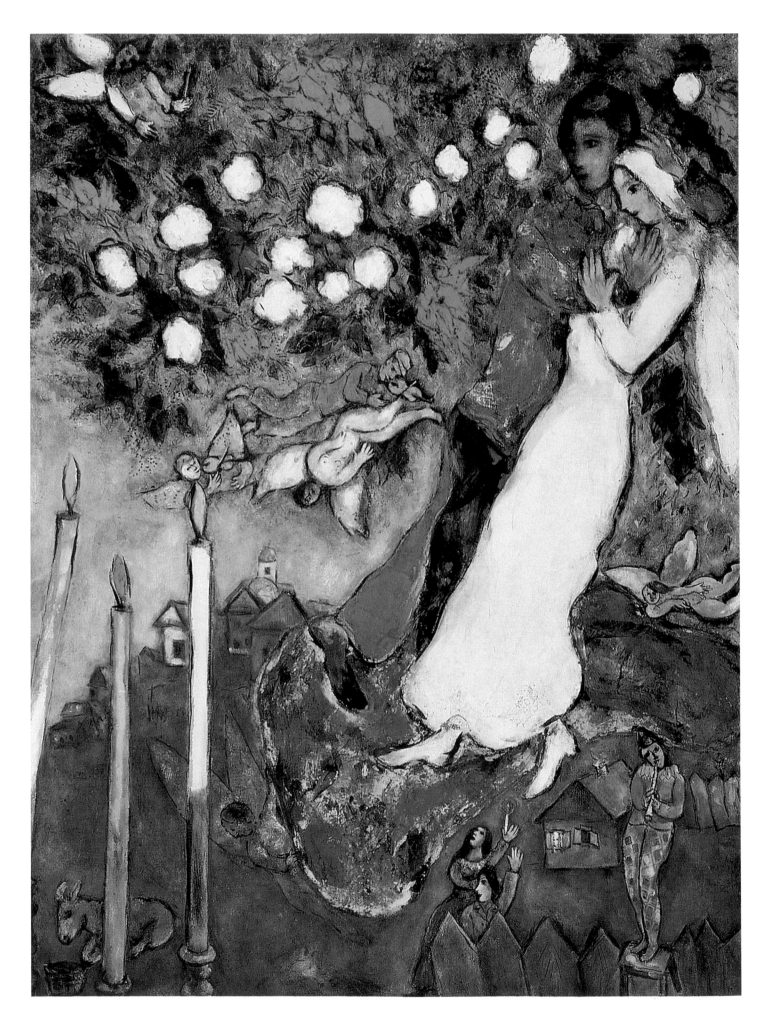

the move, so often spoken of in his paintings, was no longer merely a literary motif.

On 23 June 1941, the day Germany attacked the USSR, Chagall arrived in New York. After Paris and Berlin he now lived in the third great metropolitan melting-pot. True to his own experience, Chagall was always attracted to great cities, where diverse and exotic peoples and cultures met; they were the elixir of life to him. The family moved into a country house at Preston (Connecticut), some way out of the city, before moving into a small New York apartment.

Responding to the events of the war from a distance but with sympathy, Chagall modulated the deeply melancholy basic tone of his last French paintings in the years that followed. War and crucifixion continued to dominate his subject-matter, but the empathic intensity was somewhat diminished. It was as if the daily news of atrocities blunted Chagall's sentimental willingness to feel solidarity.

At all events, *L'Obsession* (pp. 66–7), painted in 1943, testifies to the impossibility of finding new images of concern, year in, year out. The flames pouring from the hut, the Jew with the three-branched candelabrum, the motif of flight in a cart and the menacingly fiery colours have the banality of quotations from himself, and only in the toppled crucifix, speaking of shattered hopes, does Chagall find a way of indicating the tremendous horrors of recent years. None the less, the device has something too anecdotally trivial about it, and the linking of passion and war is now too familiar to add any new dimension of pictorial sympathy to the powerful *White Crucifixion*.

This suggests one of the fundamental problems of Chagall's pictorial language: a tendency for motifs to acquire an independent existence of their own, which threatens to rob them of their expressive power. Familiar elements in his work – all the loving couples, huts, animals, and later the religious images – are deployed in new combinations to determine the character of any given painting. Like words, they are strung together into ever-new sentences, yet the many repetitions deprive them of specific meaning. Their symbolic value as representatives of another reality in a picture is levelled out; instead they become quotations from Chagall's own oeuvre. Parts of a seemingly mysterious world, they soon come to suggest nothing but their own exoticism, and the reality they are supposed to stand for becomes schematized.

Thus, in the end, a Chagall painting will convey only a mood, a mood which depends far more on the use of colour than on exact content. The

OPPOSITE:
The Three Candles, 1938–40
Oil on canvas, 127.5 x 96.5 cm (50¼ x 38 in)
Private collection

"If ever there was a moral crisis it was that of paint, matter, blood, and all their constituents, the words and the tones, all the things one makes a work of art out of, just as one makes a life. For even if you cover a canvas with thick masses of paint, irrespective of whether the outlines of shapes can be made out or not, and even if you enlist the help of words and tones, it does not necessarily follow that an authentic work of art will have been created."
MARC CHAGALL

PAGES 66–7:
L'Obsession, 1943
Oil on canvas, 77 x 108 cm (30¼ x 42½ in.)
Private collection

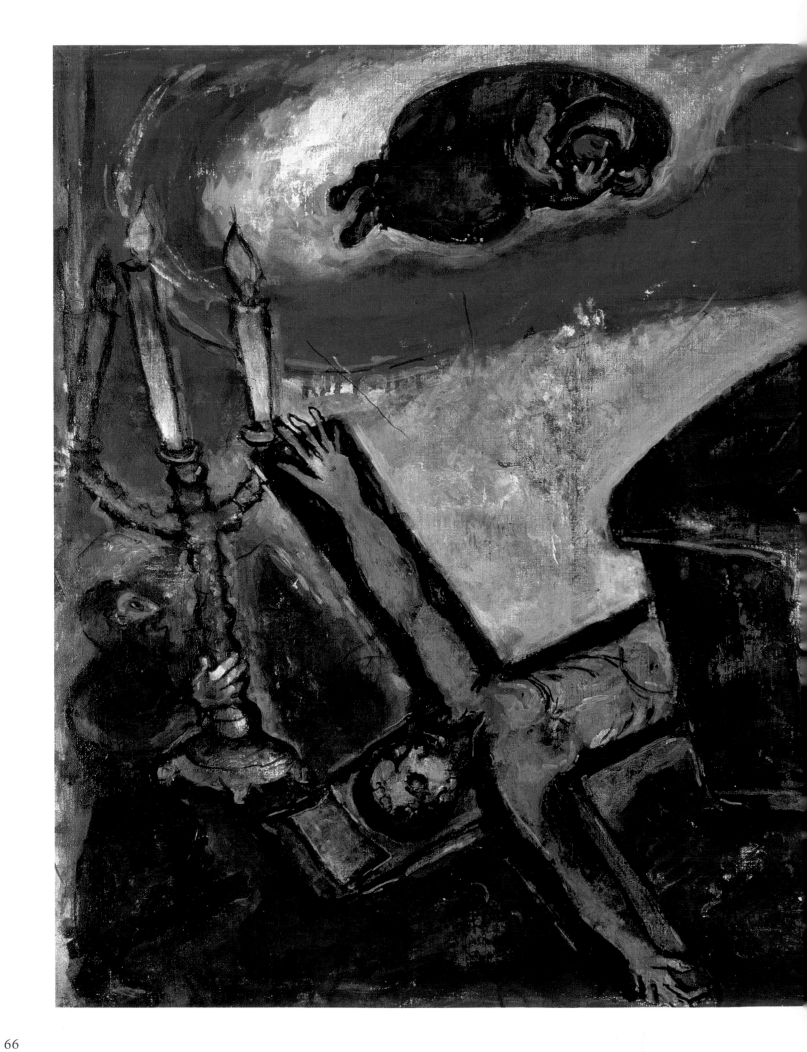

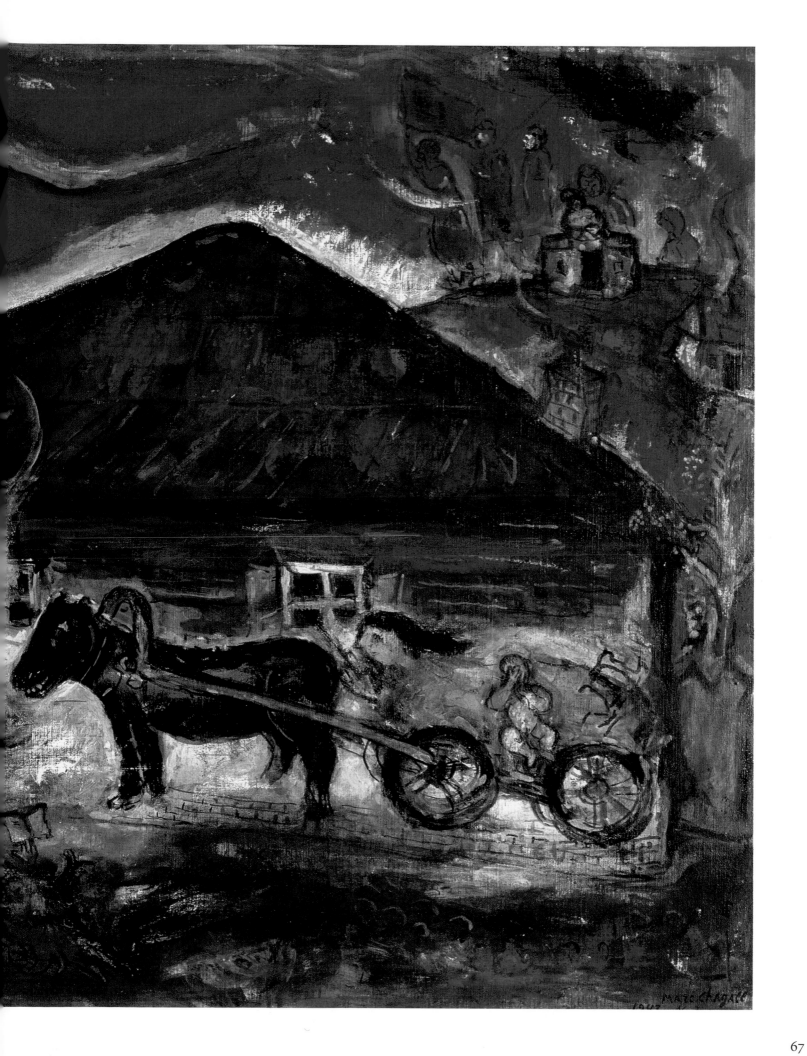

motifs merely serve a purpose of recognition, endowing the typical Chagall hallmark; and in this way Chagall's initial aura of strangeness is dispelled. The uniquely formulated appeal for tolerance and understanding became in danger of being submerged in a welter of the merely typical, and it was only Chagall's dynamic capacity for stylistic change that enabled him to keep this danger at arm's length. In this he shows himself to have been a diligent student of abstract painting: his brush-strokes and combinations of colours are the major determinations of specific content and individuality in a Chagall painting, not the thematic motifs.

The House with the Green Eye (p. 72) and *Madonna with the Sleigh* (p. 75) and, above all, *Listening to the Cock* (right) testify to this. The figure of the cockerel, distinguished from the red background only by its outline and the colourful head, incorporates two more of Chagall's exemplary motifs: the dainty position of the legs recalls the athleticism of his acrobats, while a fiddler can be found tucked away in the cock's tail-feathers. Wittily, Chagall has his cock ready to lay an egg, this image offering the same unison of male and female seen in the cow against a black background, whose head turns out to be the faces of two lovers. The crescent moon, the tree standing on its head and the hut round off this selection of Chagall's stock imagery. The ruddy dawn heralded by the cock's crow is gradually dispelling night, the province of the lovers, and this may suggest that the picture is to be read as a document of new hope, that gleam of hope Chagall felt as finally the collapse of Nazism approached.

The Darkness Has Gathered before my Eyes reads the despairing final sentence that Chagall added to Bella's book, *First Encounter*. When it was first published, in 1947, she had already been dead for three years. She had died in mysterious circumstances, of a viral infection, and all the signs that seemed to betoken a better world had gone. The muse Chagall had so often appealed to left her book as a testament, as a final spur for her husband's work.

The Wedding (p. 71), painted shortly after her death in 1944, shows the artist retelling an episode from *First Encounter*, the marriage of Bella's brother Aaron; yet the light, exhilarated tone of Bella's account, which (just like her husband's autobiography) is marked by a mood of lightheartedness and playful irony, has been displaced by sinister melancholy. Bride and groom incline towards each other almost apathetically, and the angelic musicians might well be playing a death-march as a wedding dance. Private grief had been added to the fateful course of world events, and Chagall's pictures at this time all centre upon the death of Bella.

OPPOSITE:
Listening to the Cock, 1944
Oil on canvas, 92.5 x 74.5 cm (36½ x 29¼ in.)
Art Institute of Chicago, Chicago

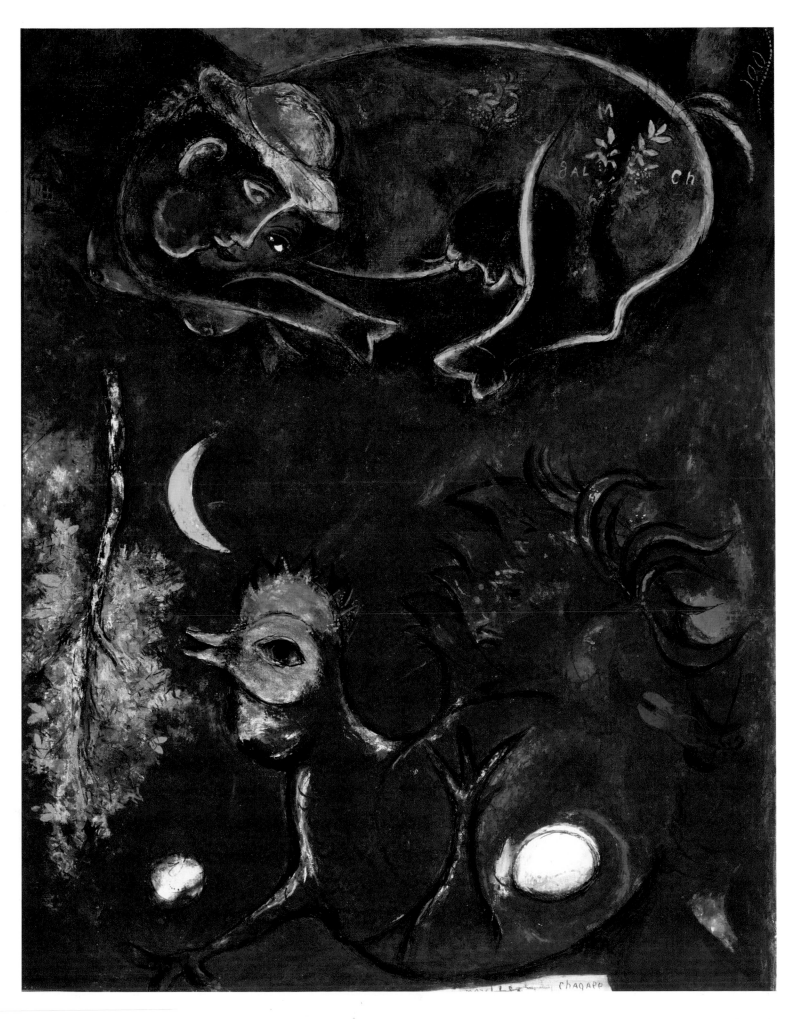

"If in some painting I have cut off the head of a cow and replaced it upside-down or have sometimes even painted the whole picture topsy-turvy, the reason was not that I wanted to create literature. I am out to introduce a psychic shock into my painting, one that is always motivated by pictorial reasoning: that is to say, a fourth dimension. An example: a street. Matisse constructs it in the spirit of Cézanne, Picasso in that of Negroes or Egyptians. I go about it differently. I have my street. In that street I place a corpse. The corpse causes psychic confusion in the street. I put a musician on a rooftop. The presence of the musician interacts with that of the corpse. Then a man sweeping the street. The image of the street-sweeper affects that of the musician. A bouquet of flowers failing down, and so forth. In this way I admit a psychic fourth dimension into pictorial representation and the two are mingled."

MARC CHAGALL

"When Chagall paints you do not know if he is asleep or awake. Somewhere or other inside his head there must be an angel."

PABLO PICASSO

OPPOSITE:
The Wedding, 1944
Oil on canvas, 99 x 74 cm (40 x 29 in.)
Ida Chagall Collection, Basle

After the liberation of Europe, Chagall ventured back into the Old World, where his career had begun for the first time in 1946. The tentatively cheerful note struck in paintings such as *Cow with Parasol* (p. 73) may derive from impressions of the return visit to Paris. A hot sun is burning in the sky, but the parasol promises relief ... relief for the cow! The artist has adopted the classic stylistic device of substitution, replacing man with an animal: it is a device that is characteristic of Chagall's art, and is used in exemplary fashion in this painting, where it contributes a great deal to the anecdotal charm that is at the core of the picture's irony. None the less, sombre colours still dominate the painting, while its humourful qualities appear to be an almost compulsive insistence on cheerfulness.

With *The Falling Angel* (p. 74), Chagall painted a last farewell to twenty-five years of artistic creativity, and the work represents both the essence of his committed involvement with the outside world and also his last word on a chronicle of increasing barbarity. It had taken Chagall twenty-five tormented years to complete the painting.

When he began it in 1923, with memories of the Russian revolution still fresh, the picture was to have included only the figures of the Jew and the Angel, and was meant as a representation of the Old Testament vindication of the presence of Evil in the world. Yet, in the years up to the painting's completion in 1947, the artist increasingly incorporated motifs reminiscent of his small Russian world, in the end even adding the images of the Madonna, and of Christ on the Cross. His Jewish vision, his personal life-story and motifs of Christian redemption are incorporated into a programmatic statement that sums up Chagall's entire oeuvre. The images have been added one to another; in their totality, and in the diversity of their associations, they represent Chagall's unceasing endeavour to locate one single, truthful, universally valid, visual formula. Its very history, its long journey half-way round the world, the whole generation required for its completion, make this picture typical of twentieth-century art, of the displacement and jeopardy that beset a work in its newly autonomous condition.

Its very history gave this picture the authority that Chagall had always aimed at, and that was commensurate with the Jewish awe of images. His own odyssey, which ended happily with his final return to France in summer 1948, had also been the odyssey of his work from a very early stage, ever since Walden's Berlin exhibition.

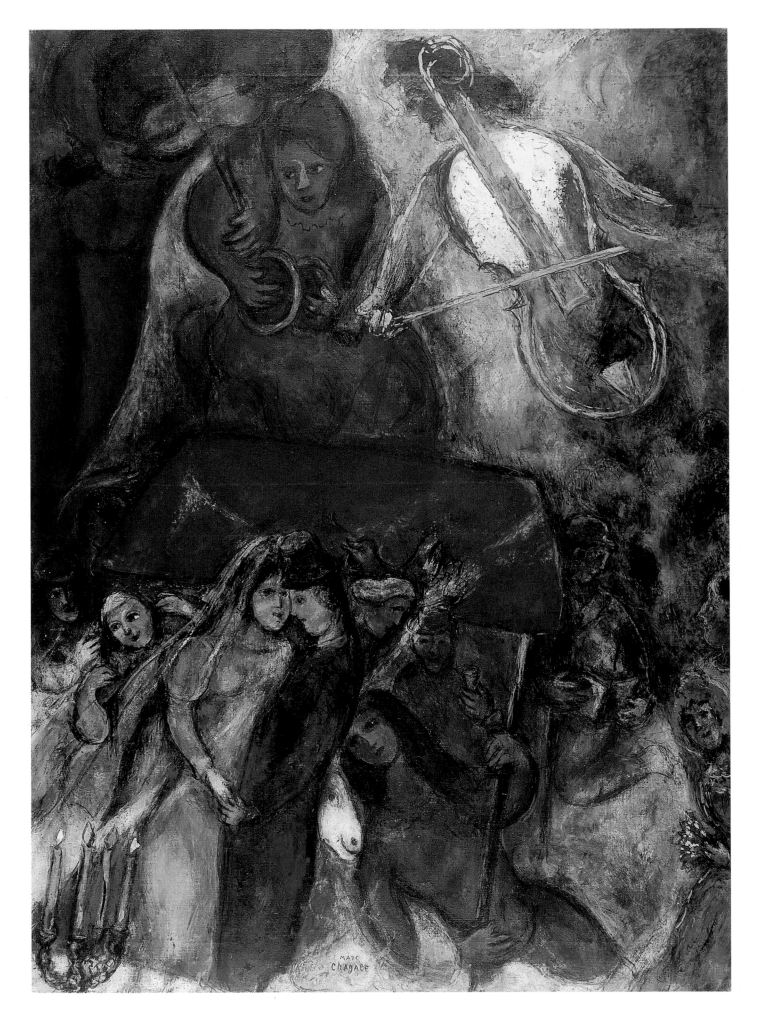

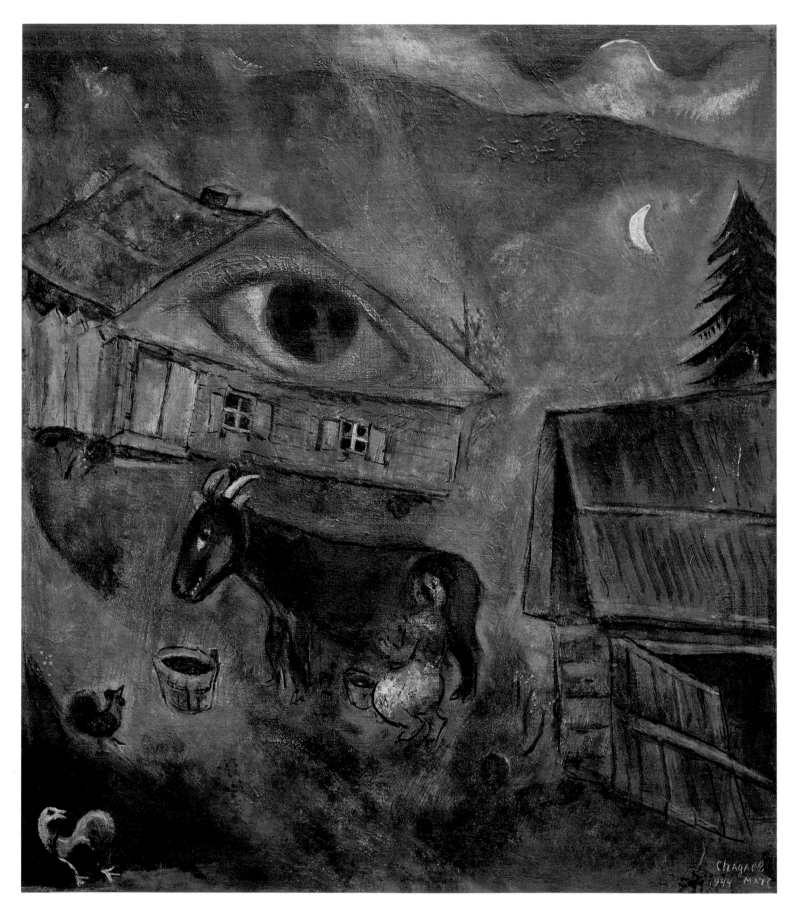

The House with the Green Eye, 1944
Oil on canvas, 58 x 51 cm (22¾ x 20 in.)
Private collection

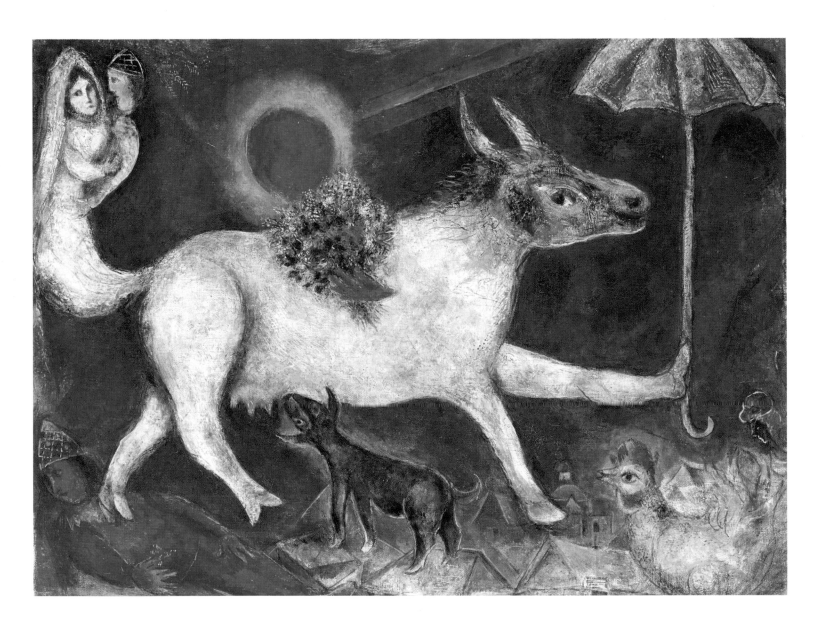

Cow with Parasol, 1946
Oil on canvas, 75 x 106.6 cm (29½ x 42 in.)
Richard S. Zeisler Collection, New York

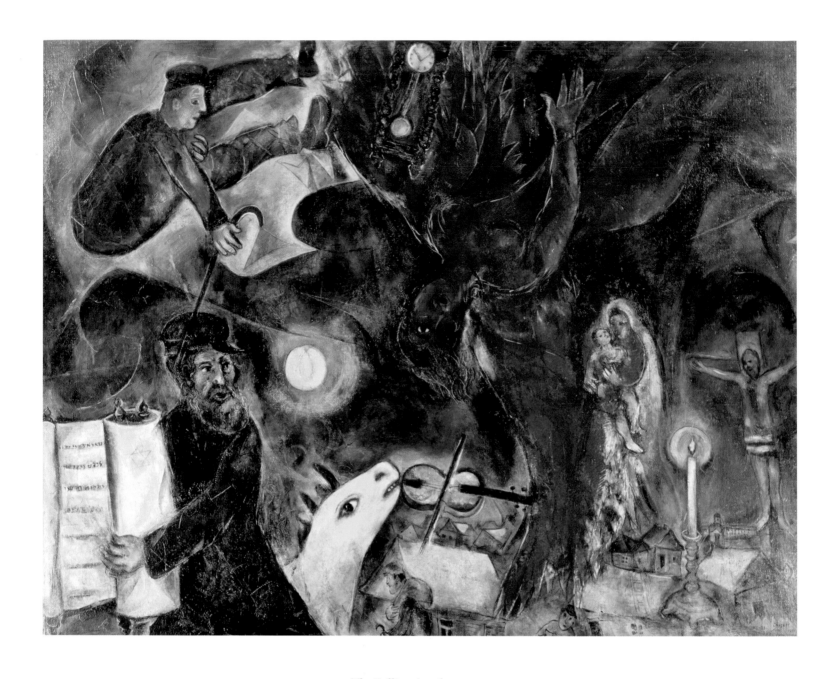

The Falling Angel, 1923–47
Oil on canvas, 148 x 189 cm (58¼ x 74½ in.)
Kunstmuseum, Basle

OPPOSITE:
Madonna with the Sleigh, 1947
Oil on canvas, 97 x 80 cm (38¼ x 31½ in.)
Stedelijk Museum, Amsterdam

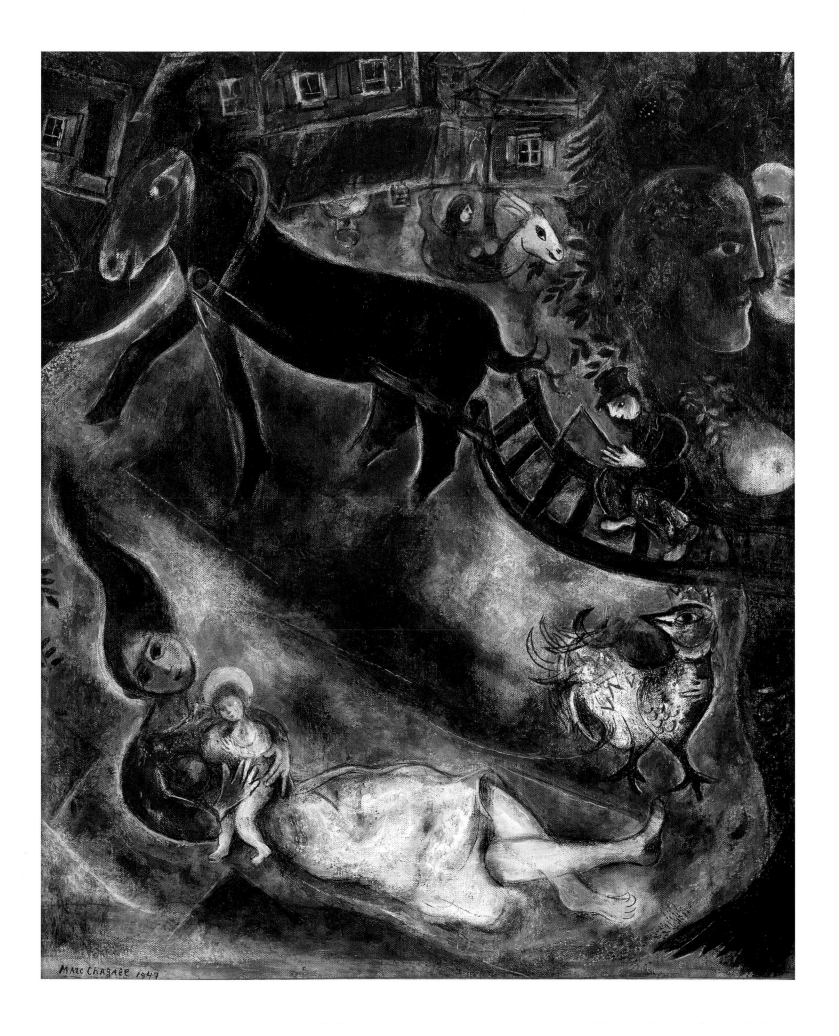

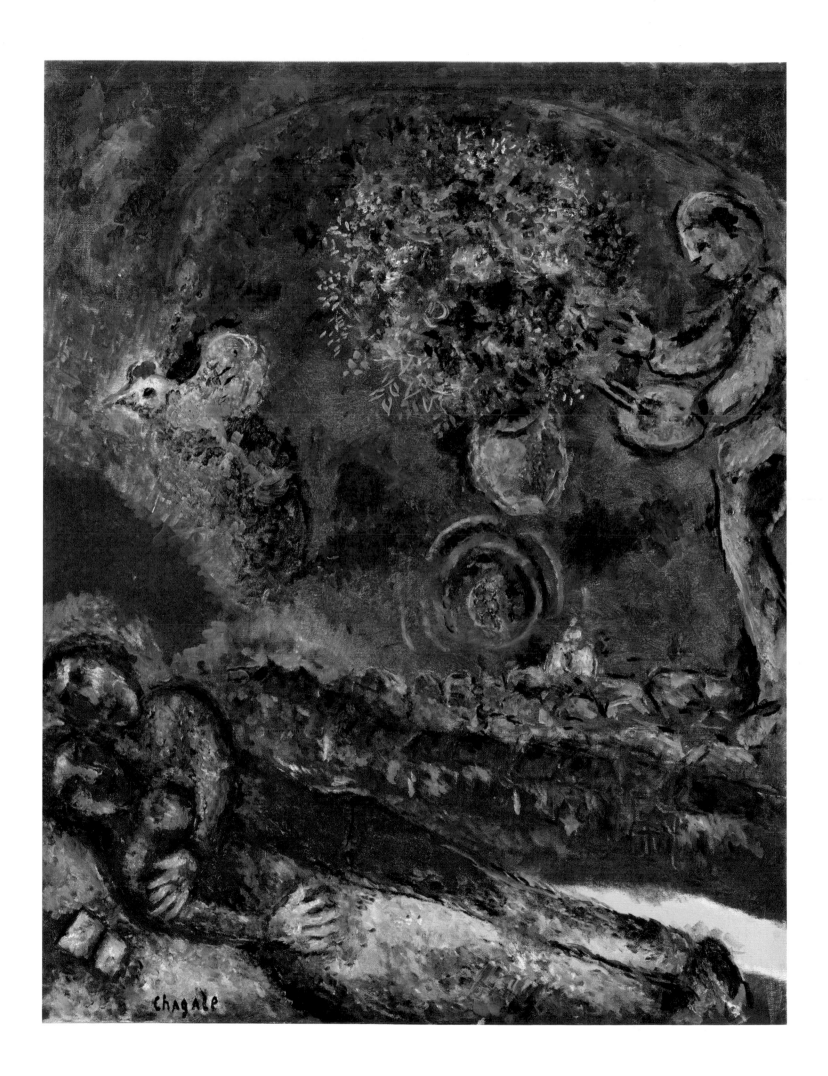

The Late Work
1948–1985

After his return to France, Chagall's work still remained a poetic metaphor for his turbulent life-history, a balancing-act negotiating dream and reality, an adventure of the imagination that made the invisible visible, and thus real. His late work, however, seemed gradually to achieve distance from the twin starting-points in his artistic life, namely the orthodox Jewish tradition and Russian folklore.

His subject-matter, which was taken from his cultural knowledge of a small Russian village, was superseded by the use of motifs from Greek mythology, Christian belief and his own everyday experience. Thus his choice of subjects underwent a cautious change, and furthermore the content of his repeatedly deployed symbols was worn away in the course of time. And after 1947 Chagall's links to avant-garde art increasingly weakened almost to the point of non-existence, so that his visual terms came to seem, rather than a matter of personal preferences developed over the years, a wish to maintain connections with the latest formal tendencies in the art scene. But it was not only the artistic market-place that Chagall avoided. More and more, he liked to withdraw completely into his private life, and the turbulence of his earlier life was now a thing of the past: in 1950 he moved into a house at Saint-Jean-Cap-Ferrat, and two years later married for the second time. His new beloved was a Russian woman, Valentina Brodsky, whom Chagall tenderly nicknamed "Vava". This domestic bliss was to be Chagall's touchstone during this period when his art, and the artist himself, were becoming objects of mounting public interest.

Despite his growing fame, his pictures nevertheless remained as intimate and as naïvely unworldly in his later years as they had been at the outset. *Couple on a Red Background* (left) was painted as late as 1983. The man, meaning to win over the woman with tenderness, is placing his arm about the woman's breast, gently inclining his head, trying to look her in the eye, while she, still hesitant, is turning away and looking out at us, as if we, by looking at the scene, were disturbing the couple's loving tryst.

The red, which veritably glows in the couple, is matched by a cool blue, and in it, at the right-hand margin, we see the painter himself with a palette in his left hand. It appears as if the vase of flowers is slipping from his open arms, just as the book is being dropped by the lovers. The blue oval echoes the shape of the palette and the bunch of flowers and the bird are no more than abstract dabs of paint.

The images in a painting done exactly thirty years previously, one of a Paris series, are strikingly similar (see p. 78): once again the heart of the composition

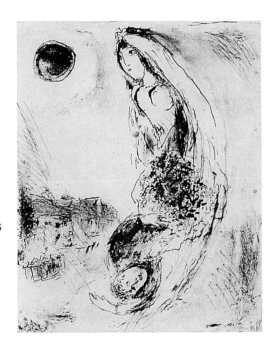

The Half-Moon Couple, 1951–2
Lithograph, 41.5 x 34.3 cm (16¼ x 13½ in.)

OPPOSITE:
Couple on a Red Background, 1983
Oil on canvas, 81 x 65.5 cm (32 x 25¾ in.)
Christie's Images

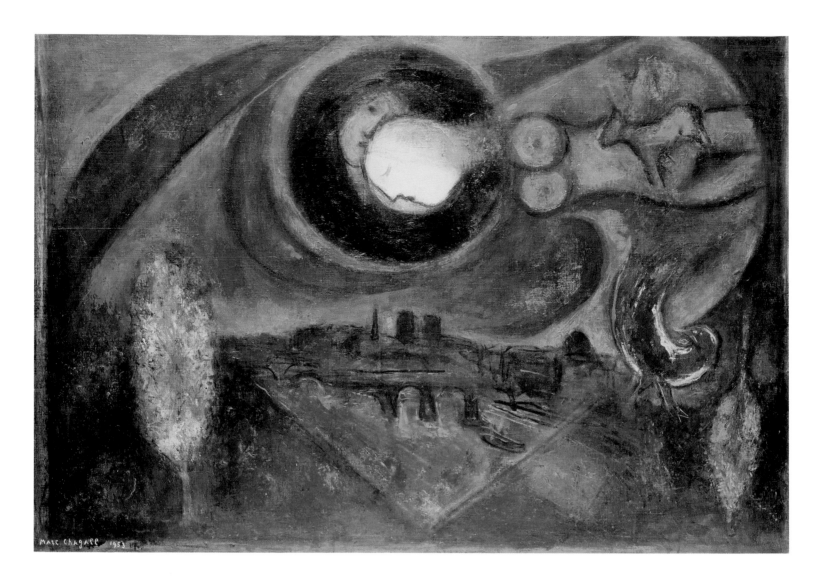

Le Quai de Bercy, 1953
Oil on canvas, 65 x 95 cm (25½ x 37½ in.)
Ida Chagall Collection, Basle

"If a symbol should be discovered in a painting
of mine, it was not my intention. It is a result I
did not seek. It is something that may be found
afterwards, and which can be interpreted
according to taste."

MARC CHAGALL

is occupied by a loving couple, once again there is a bird, and the tree to the left
is coloured like a bouquet of flowers. However, Chagall is not merely re-using
the same motifs decade after decade; a second parallel between the 1953 and
1983 paintings can also be established.

If the seemingly abstract shape of the blue area in the later painting is a larger
version of the artist's palette, in the earlier painting we can make out a compara-
ble suggestion of an outsize heart. The tip touches the lower-margin of the
painting; the heart itself is squarely in the centre of the picture. One diagonal
runs to the left into the tree, first serving to indicate the river and the side of the
heart; a second line crosses the river to the right and, in the upper half of the
painting, is rounded into the typical stylized heart-shape. The symbol of love
embraces a loving couple.

In his late work, Chagall was frequently able to endow shapes dictated by
technical – that is to say, abstract – reasons with pictorial functions. What
seems at first glance to be an arrangement of lines and zones determined along
compositional principles turns out to be a sign emphasizing the meaning of the
picture, such as the heart. In this way Chagall puts behind him the ideas of the
Cubists and the visual concepts of Delaunay, who had once influenced him. In
earlier days, his wish to base a painting wholly on formal principles, to enmesh
it in a purely abstract net, so to speak, was at odds with his aim to present iden-
tifiable objects.

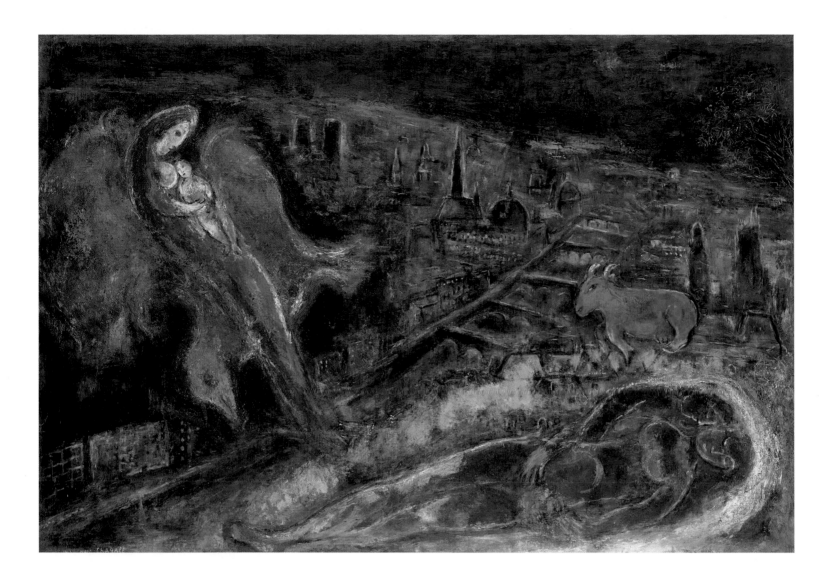

This new function of form as a vehicle of a painting's content is matched in many works by a newly liberated use of colour. Slightly late in the day, Chagall took to the kind of *tachiste* painting that Jackson Pollock had initiated in 1947 with his first drip paintings.

In *Bridges over the Seine* (above), for instance, the area of blue can no longer be wholly identified with an object in the composition. On the one hand, it fully covers the reclining couple; yet, on the other, it spreads beyond them and becomes a sort of aura about the embracing lovers. In this, as in all his other paintings that betray the influence of American abstract expressionism, Chagall's brush-work is far from spontaneous; it simply reinforces the impression of naïve innocence that Chagall, ever subtle in his approach, had always called forth in his figures.

The theme of colour grown autonomous is varied in a number of paintings of flowers at this period, such as *Le Champ de Mars* (p. 81). The floral motifs afford Chagall a welcome opportunity to indulge in masterly craftsmanship: colour values are savoured, tonal qualities painstakingly harmonized and colour contrasts relished in. These floral elements in the paintings are havens of pure painting: surrounded by work no less delicately painted, but anchored to a greater extent in the representation of the actual.

A good example of Chagall's use of this new autonomy of colour as a kind of "first aid" for those who view his work is *The Concert* (p. 82), painted in 1957. A

Bridges over the Seine, 1954
Oil on canvas, 111.5 x 163.5 cm (44 x 64¾ in.)
Kunsthalle, Hamburg

"The habit of ignoring Nature is deeply implanted in our times. This attitude reminds me of people who never look you in the eye; I find them disturbing and always have to look away."

MARC CHAGALL

79

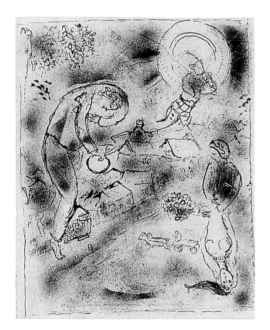

The Roofs, 1956
Lithograph, 55 x 41 cm (21½ x 16 in.)

"I do not know (and who can predict?) what external form or inner character French art will have in the future, once France has recovered from this horrible tragedy ... I am convinced that France will again bring forth marvels to follow in the footsteps of the great masters of the past. Let us all believe in the genius of France."

MARC CHAGALL

OPPOSITE:
Le Champ de Mars, 1954–5
Oil on canvas, 149.5 x 105 cm (58¾ x 41¼ in.)
Museum Folkwang, Essen

boat with a couple on board is drifting along a river, with a city on the bank to the right and a group of musicians to the left. The lovers' naked bodies are shrouded in a glowing red that extends upwards beyond their heads. Parallel to this band of colour are two other strips of blue that run from the water to the musicians. These bands suggest that the boat is moving from the bottom-right to upper-left; so this romantic boating trip, under a full moon, proves in fact to be a voyage from the city cloaked in cool blue to a higher sphere peopled by heavenly musicians.

The Eiffel Tower, the Arc de Triomphe and Notre-Dame reveal the city to be Paris, the city where Chagall had his atelier before the war at a time when it was still what it was no longer to be in the aftermath: a great art metropolis. Like many fellow-artists, Chagall had turned his back on Paris, and the Côte d'Azur had become a little Montparnasse. It was an apt setting for Chagall, and he was not to leave the region; indeed, in 1967 he built a house large enough for his requirements at Saint-Paul-de-Vence. It contained three studios, one for graphic work, one for drawing, and a third for painting and large-scale designs.

Not long before this final move he completed work on *Exodus* (p. 83). The title alludes to the exodus of the Israelites from Egypt in 1200 BC, as recounted in the Old Testament. After crossing the Red Sea in miraculous manner, Moses, the leader, was handed down the Ten Commandments. In the painting he is seen standing at bottom-right, holding the tablets with the Commandments, which he has just received from the Hand of God. Beyond him, a vast crowd is pouring out of the picture's distant depths. These are the people of Israel on the way to their own land, a story that is told as a parable in the Bible and that was also historical reality throughout the Second World War until the establishment of the State of Israel in 1948. So Chagall sees it – and in the process, in his familiar way, he mixes up the various historical levels and literary sources.

Thoughts of flight and exile reappear in the painting *War* (p. 84). A wretched and drastically overloaded cart is slowly putting the burning city behind it. A man is plodding along behind the cart, a sack over his shoulder, saving his worldly goods from the flames. Most of the people here can only just save their lives, though, and cling to each other in confused despair. The people and animals that have remained in the city are helplessly at the mercy of the all-consuming inferno. Chagall feelingly portrays the sufferings people underwent during the war, and by adding to this scenario of cruelty and violence a crucifixion scene in the upper right he elevates the victims of the war to the status of martyrs, who – although themselves guiltless – are forced to bear the burden of expiation.

Modern history paintings of this order were few, and they were not so much reflections of precise historical events as examinations of human suffering; however, Chagall's portraits at this time were even fewer. His two wives were the only people he honoured with portraits after he left Russia. In 1966 he painted *Vava* (p. 85), his chosen one, seated on a chair, her left arm resting on the back. In front of her float a couple of lovers, presumably to remove any doubts the wife might have had about her husband's affection. In the background we see the painter's traditional repertoire of Eiffel Tower, a red animal's head, a village street, but here they suggest the interior of a studio where Vava, Chagall's muse, is posing in front of the very paintings she inspired him to create.

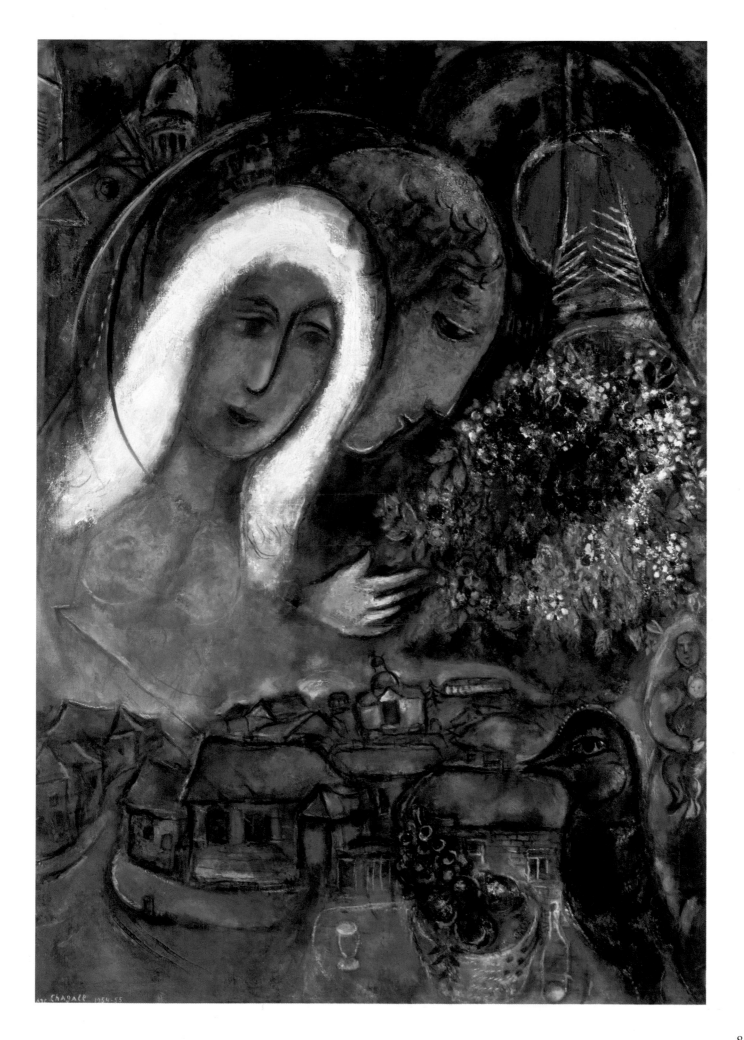

The Concert, 1957
Oil on canvas, 140 x 239.5 cm (55 x 94¼ in.)
Private collection

"For me, the circus is a magical show, like a world that comes into being and then is gone again," declared Chagall, writing of a world that is very closely related to that which many of his paintings, such as *The Large Circus* (p. 87) and *The Grand Parade* (p. 90), pay homage to. Boisterous merriment and music, a showcase of magic and freakish oddities, a place where laws have ceased to apply – the description is as applicable to Chagall's pictures as to the world of the circus. When the painter presents the happy goings-on in the arena, he is expressing in concrete terms the fantasies that otherwise exist only in his dreams, expressing them in terms of a corresponding reality. In the Big Top, a man who can fly is quite simply a trapeze artiste.

And in *The Fall of Icarus* (p. 88), the man who so wondrously has wings is not a product of the painter's imagination but instead derives from Greek myth. Icarus and his father Dedalus built a flying-machine to escape from their imprisonment on the island of Crete; but the son, rather too impetuously, flew too close to the sun and the wax that held his wings together melted, so that he lost them and plummeted into the sea. Chagall's painting relocates the scene of the story, so that it now takes place before the attentive eyes of countless onlookers. The peace of the village is profoundly disturbed by the historic event. While *The Fall of Icarus* is painted in unusually bright colours to emphasize the special role of the sun in the old tale, in *The Myth of Orpheus* (p. 89), by contrast, dark shades predominate. The Greek hero of the myth was compelled to descend into the Underworld to reclaim his beloved Eurydice.

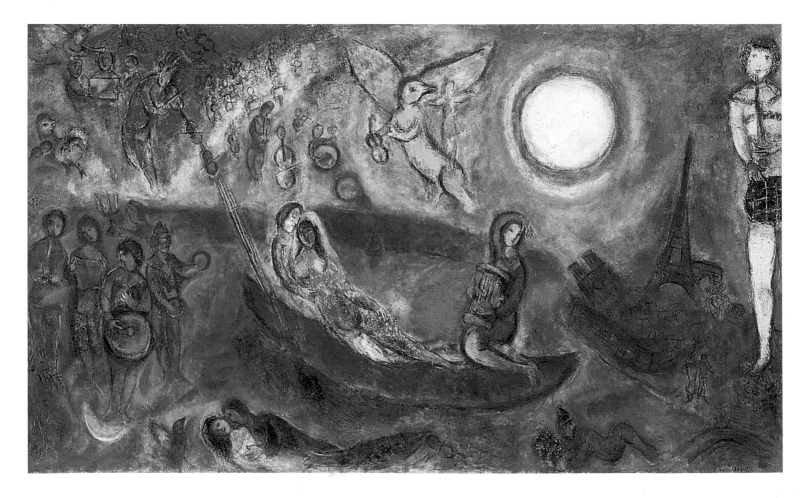

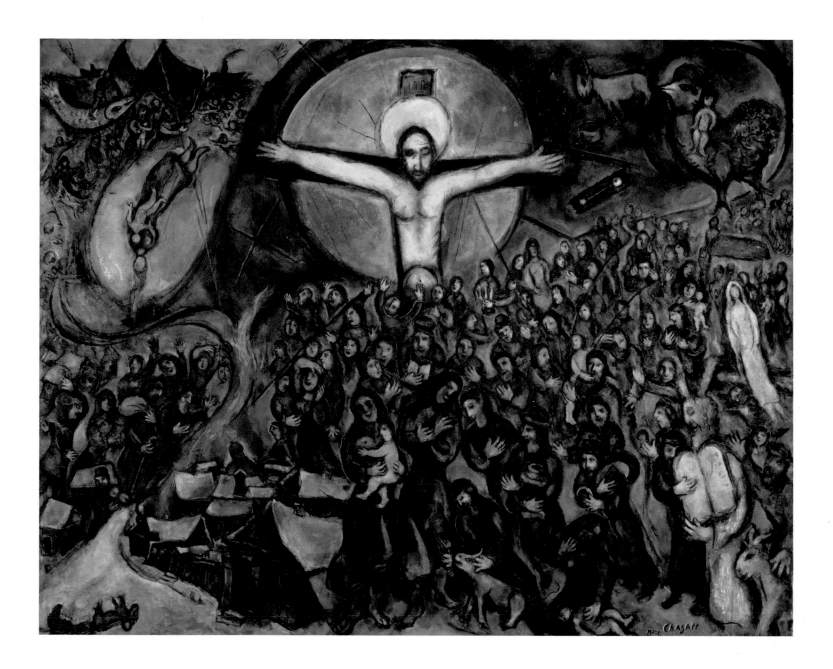

Chagall always aimed to create great art, and in every period of his creative life he approached his self-imposed aim in a different way. In his late work – apart from a number of lithographs, such as the famous Bible illustrations (which appeared in 1957) and *Daphnis and Chloë* (1961) – the major challenge to his energies was offered by monumental murals, mosaics, tapestries and stained-glass windows.

In rapid succession, Chagall undertook the following commissions (to list only the most important of them): the interior of the church of Plateau d'Assy in Savoy (1957); windows for Metz Cathedral (beginning in 1958); a mural for the foyer of the theatre in Frankfurt (1959); windows for the synagogue of the University Clinic in Jerusalem (1962); windows in the United Nations building in New York, and ceiling paintings in the Paris Opera House (1964); murals in Tokyo and Tel Aviv, and for the Metropolitan Opera in New York (1965); murals for the new parliament building in Jerusalem (1966); mosaics for the University of Nice (1968); stained-glass windows for the Minster of Our Lady in Zurich (1970); mosaics for the Chagall Museum in Nice (1971); windows for Reims Cathedral; mosaics for the First National Bank in Chicago (1974); and windows

Exodus, 1952-66
Oil on canvas, 130 x 162 cm (51¼ x 63¾ in.)
Private collection

"Changes in societal structure and in art would possess more credibility if they had their origins in the soul and spirit. If people read the words of the prophets with closer attention, they would find the keys to life."

MARC CHAGALL

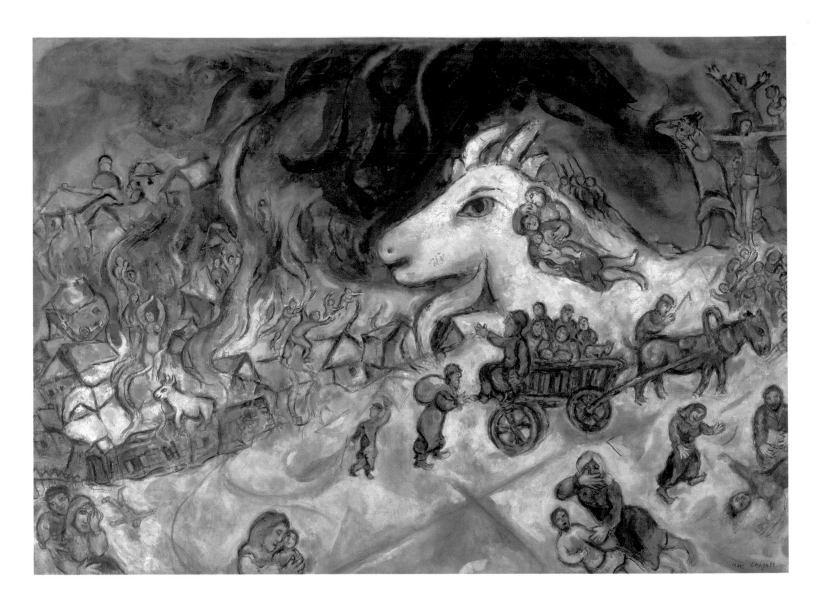

War, 1964–6
Oil on canvas, 163 x 231 cm (64¼ x 91 in.)
Kunsthaus, Zurich

OPPOSITE:
Portrait of Vava, 1966
Oil on canvas, 92 x 65 cm (36¼ x 25½ in.)
Private collection

for St Stephen's in Mainz (beginning in 1978). Neither Chagall nor those who gave him his commissions felt that belonging to a specific religious community need play a decisive part. The artist used his talents equally for synagogues and cathedrals. After all, even the Communist Léger had been allowed to paint a chapel interior!

And so had Matisse. When Chagall viewed the decorations Matisse created for the church at Vence, however, he felt that they were unsuited to prayer; his own style was far better for tasks of this nature. It was essential to strike a universal religious note, and the specific images tended to be of secondary significance. The windows he made for the church of All Saints in Tudeley in the English county of Kent, for example, allude to the death of a girl only incidentally (see p. 91). The girl had drowned in an accident at sea and her parents commissioned the windows and so a private tragedy was heightened, in Chagall's work, by the use of his usual figures and religious symbols. What most engages the eye, however, are motifs taken from Nature, and they, together with the blue that floods everything, achieve the desired mystical mood that prompts us to contemplation and penitence.

No other twentieth-century artist had Chagall's gift for harmonizing what were thought to be irreconcilable opposites. He bridged gaps that had been widening for centuries between different religious communities and ideologies –

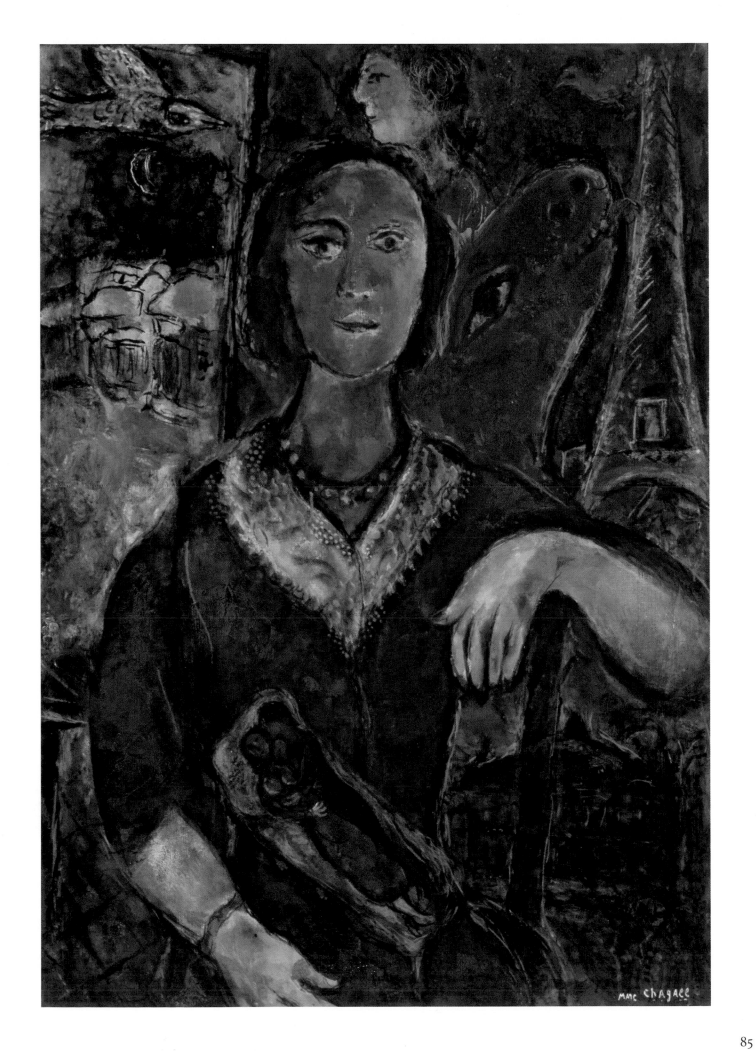

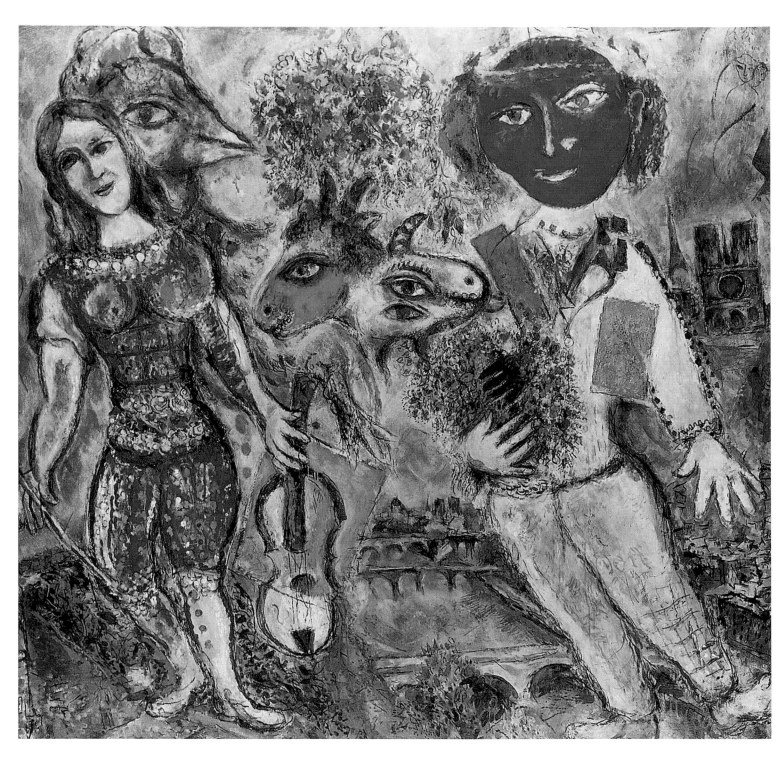

The Players, 1968
Oil on canvas, 150 x 160 cm (59 x 63 in.)
Private collection

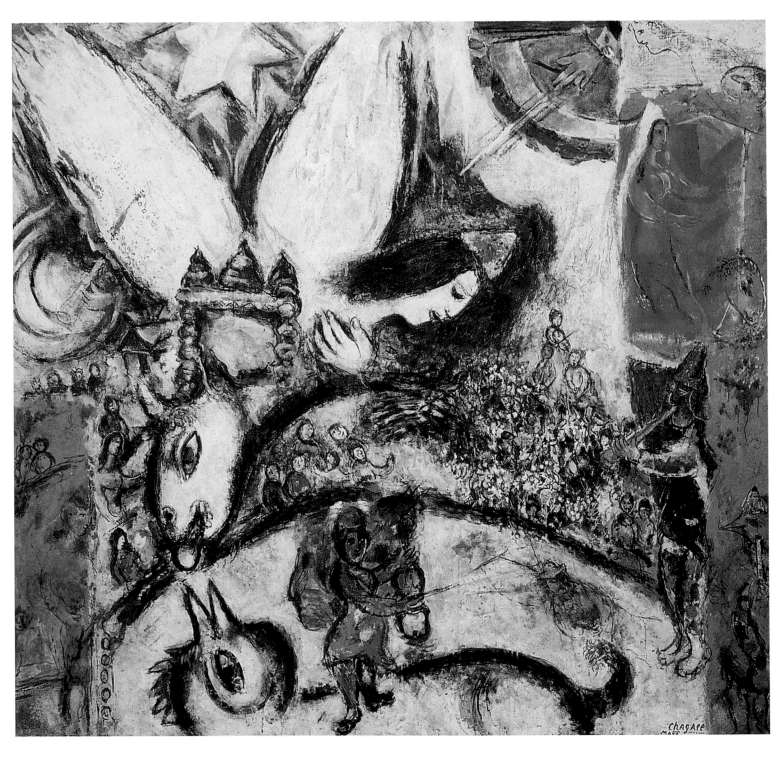

The Large Circus, 1968
Oil on canvas, 170 x 160 cm (67 x 63 in.)
Private collection

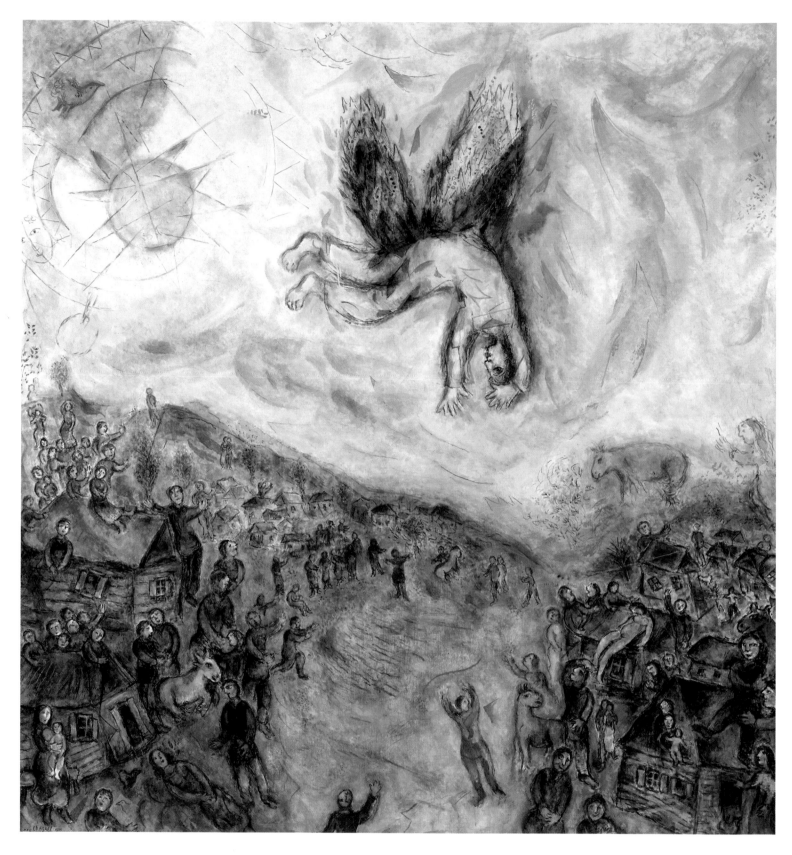

The Fall of Icarus, 1975
Oil on canvas, 213 x 198 cm (83¾ x 78 in.)
Musée national d'art moderne. Centre Georges Pompidou, Paris

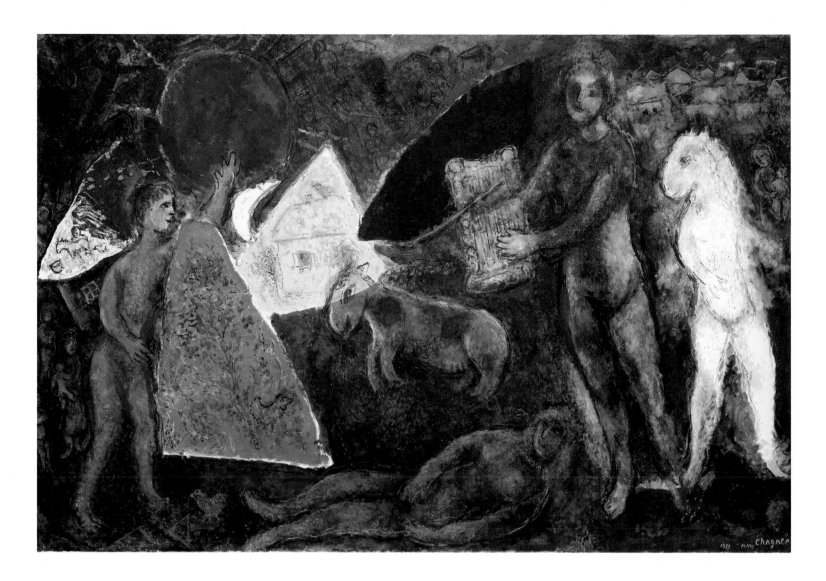

not least, artistic ideologies. It was this power to integrate that enabled him to satisfy the public's longing for one peaceful family of humanity, one world of brotherly peace.

The soothing message was no less than Arcadia, paradise and Elysium in one. And Marc Chagall, forever travelling between different worlds, was the messenger.

The Myth of Orpheus, 1977
Oil on canvas, 97 x 146 cm (38¼ x 57½ in.)
Private collection

"We all know that a good person can be a bad artist. But no one will ever be a genuine artist unless he is a great human being and thus also a good one."

MARC CHAGALL

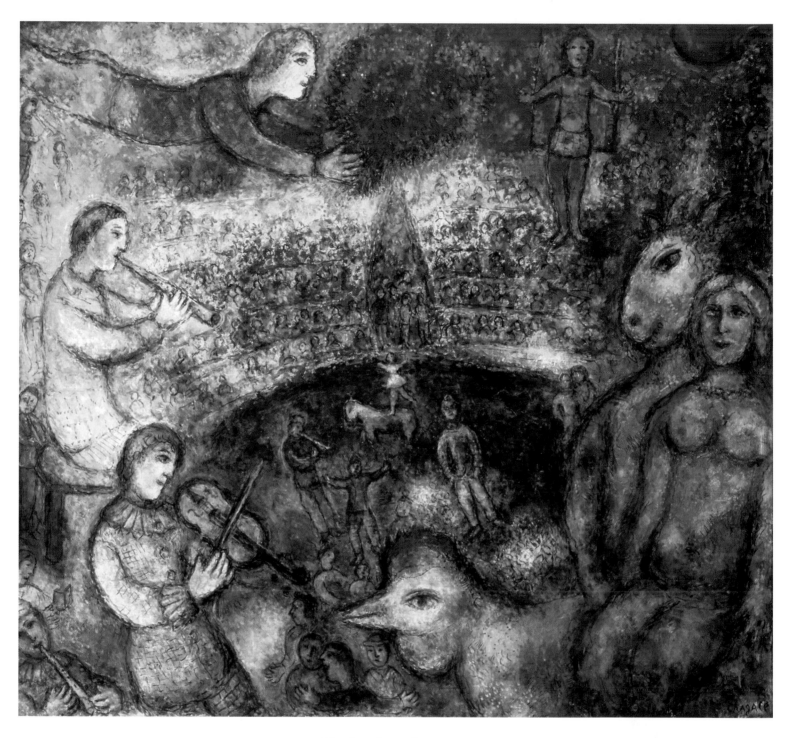

The Grand Parade, 1979–80
Oil on canvas, 119 x 132 cm (46¾ x 52 in.)
Christie's Images

OPPOSITE:
Angels and Animals, 1978
Stained-glass window, 157.5 x 40 cm (62 x 15¾ in.)
All Saints' Church, choir, south wall, Tudeley (Kent)

Trees and Angels, 1978
Stained glass window, 131.5 x 34.5 cm (55¾ x 13½ in.)
All Saints' Church, choir, south wall, Tudeley (Kent)

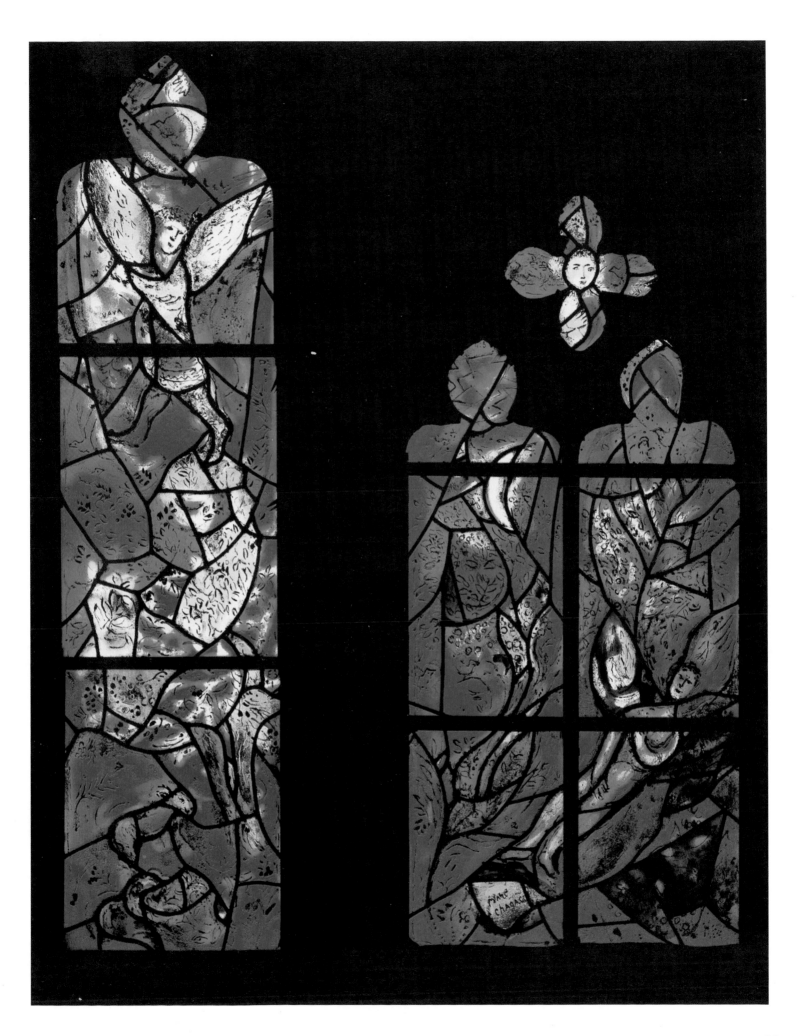

Marc Chagall 1887–1985
A Chronology

1887 Marc Chagall is born in Vitebsk, White Russia, on 7 July, the oldest of nine children, of Jewish parents. His mother, Feige-Ita, is a simple woman. His father, Sachar, works in a herring depot.

1906 Finishes school and attends painter Yehuda Pen's studio as his pupil.

1907 With his friend Mekler he goes to St Petersburg and studies at the Imperial Society for the Promotion of the Arts.

1908 Changes to the Svanseva School, run by Léon Bakst, and remains there until 1910.

1909 Repeated visits to Vilebsk, where he gets to know Bella Rosenfeld, daughter of a jeweller, who will become his wife.

1910 Goes to Paris with funds given by a patron. Fascinated by the intense use of colour in the work of Van Gogh and the Fauves. *Birth* (p. 11).

1911 Exhibits *I and the Village* (p. 21) at the Salon des Indépendants. Moves into a studio at La Ruche, where Léger, Modigliani and Soutine also live. Friendship with Léger, Cendrars, Apollinaire and Delaunay.

1912 Exhibits at the Salon des Indépendants and the Autumn Salon. *The Cattle Dealer* (p. 31).

1913 Through Apollinaire he becomes acquainted with the Berlin art dealer Herwarth Walden and exhibits in an autumn show in Berlin.

1914 First solo exhibition, at Der Sturm, Walden's Berlin gallery. Travels from Berlin to Vitebsk, where he is surprised by the outbreak of the First World War. Almost all the works left behind in Paris and Berlin are lost. In St Petersburg he does war work.

1915 On 25 July he marries Bella Rosenfeld in Vitebsk. In the autumn he moves to Petrograd. *The Poet Reclining* (p. 40) and *The Birthday* (p. 38).

1916 Birth of daughter, Ida. Exhibitions in Moscow and Petrograd.

1917–18 Chagall is made Fine Arts Commissar for the Vitebsk region, to which he returns. There he founds a modern school of art, where Lissitzky and Malevich also teach. He arranges celebrations for the first anniversary of the October Revolution. The first monograph on Chagall is published. After a quarrel with Malevich he leaves the academy. *Cemetery Gates* (p. 45).

The Chagall family in Vitebsk (Marc is standing second from right).

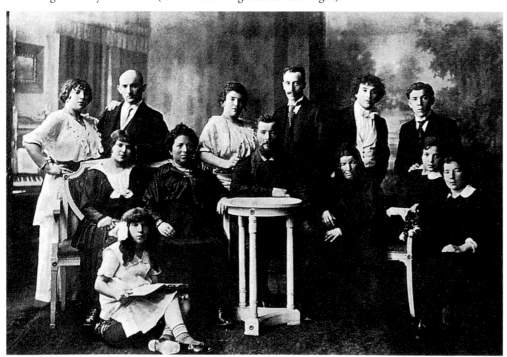

Chagall in 1925.

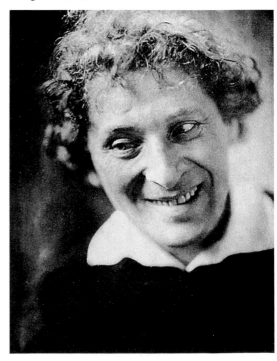

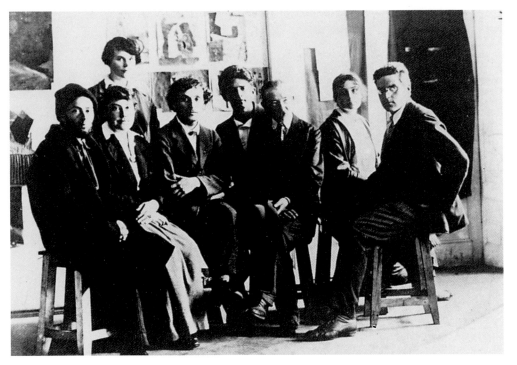

Chagall (seated, third from left) with the committee of the Vitebsk academy. El Lissitzky is on the far left. Third from right is Yehuda Pen, Chagall's first teacher in Vitebsk. Summer 1919.

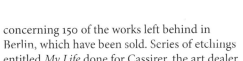

Chagall working on the design for a mural for the Jewish Theatre in Moscow, c. 1920–1.

1919–20 Exhibits in the first official show of revolutionary art in Petrograd; the government buys twelve of his paintings. Moves to Moscow and designs murals and decorations for the Jewish Theatre.

1921 Works as a drawing instructor at the Malachovka home for war orphans near Moscow.

1922 Leaves Russia for good and travels to Paris, his wife and daughter following. Legal case

concerning 150 of the works left behind in Berlin, which have been sold. Series of etchings entitled *My Life* done for Cassirer, the art dealer.

1923 Makes his home in Paris. Illustrates Gogol's *Dead Souls* for the publisher Vollard (not published until 1948).

1924 First retrospective in Paris. Summer vacation in Brittany.

1925 Illustrations for La Fontaine's *Fables*, commissioned by Vollard (but not published until 1952). *Peasant Life* (p. 53).

1926–7 First solo exhibition in New York. Does 19 gouaches for a circus portfolio. Summer in the Auvergne.

1928 Works on the *Fables*. Summer in Oret, winter in Savoy.

1930 Commissioned to illustrate the Bible for Vollard. *The Acrobat* (p. 59).

1931 His autobiography, *My Life*, is published in Bella's translation. Together with his family he

Chagall with his palette, 1925.

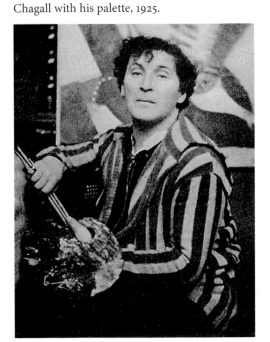

Chagall giving art classes at the Malachovka home for war orphans near Moscow in 1920.

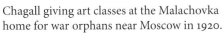

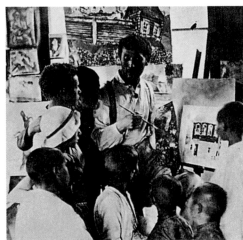

With Bella, before leaving for Paris, 1922.

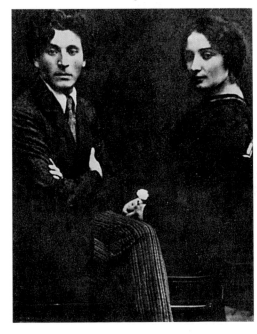

travels to the opening of the museum in Tel Aviv, and studies biblical landscapes in Palestine, Syria and Egypt.

1932 Travels to Holland. Sees Rembrandt's etchings for the first time.

1933 Large retrospective show in the Basle Kunsthalle.

1934–5 Travels to Spain. Impressed by El Greco. Travels to Vilna and Warsaw, and senses the dangers that threaten the Jews.

1937 Becomes a French citizen. A number of his paintings are included in the Nazi display of "degenerate" art – 59 are confiscated. Travels to Florence. *The Revolution* (p. 61).

1938 His paintings of the Crucifixion recall the sufferings of his people. Exhibits in Brussels. *White Crucifixion* (p. 63).

1939–40 Receives the Carnegie Painting Prize. When the War breaks out he moves to the Loire, taking his paintings with him, and later to Gordes, in unoccupied Provence.

1941 Travels to Marseilles, and from there to New York at the invitation of the Museum of Modern Art, where he arrives on 23 June, the day the Germans invade Russia.

1942 Spends summer in Mexico, designing the set for Massine's Tchaikovsky ballet *Aleko* for the New York Metropolitan Opera.

1943 Summer at Cranberry Lake near New York. Chagall is deeply moved by the course of the war in Europe. *L'Obsession* (pp. 66–7).

1944 Bella dies of a viral infection on 2 September. For months, Chagall is unable to work. *The House with the Green Eye* (p. 72).

Chagall in 1930.

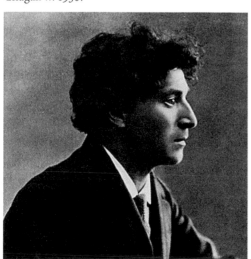

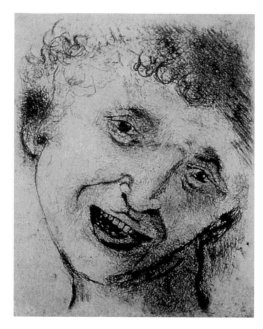

Self-portrait, laughing, c. 1924–5
Etching and cold needle, 27.7 x 21.7 cm
Private collection

1945 Resumes painting for the first time since the death of Bella. Designs sets and costumes for Stravinsky's ballet *The Firebird* at the Metropolitan Opera.

1946 Retrospective at the Museum of Modern Art and then in Chicago. First post-war trip to Paris. Coloured lithographs for *The Arabian Nights*.

1947 Exhibition at the Musée national d'art moderne in Paris and then in Amsterdam and London. *Madonna with the Sleigh* (p. 75).

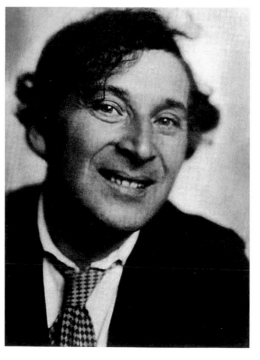

1948 Final return to Paris in August. Lives in Orgeval near Saint-Germain-en-Laye. Wins First Prize for Graphic Art at the 25th Biennale in Venice.

1949 Moves to Saint-Jean-Cap-Ferrat on the Côte d'Azur. Murals for the Watergate Theatre in London.

1950 Settles in Vence. First ceramic works. Retrospectives in Zurich and Berne.

1951 Travels to Jerusalem for the opening of an exhibition. First sculptures.

1952 On 12 July he marries Juli Valentina (Vava) Brodsky. The publisher Teriade commissions lithographs for *Daphnis and Chloë*. La Fontaine's *Fables* are published. First visit to Greece with Vava.

1953 Exhibition in Turin. Series of Paris paintings. *Le Quai de Bercy* (p. 78), *Bridges over the Seine* (p. 79).

1954 Second trip to Greece. Works on *Daphnis and Chloë*.

1955/56 Exhibitions in Hanover, Basle and Berne. "Circus" series of lithographs.

1957 Travels to Haifa for the opening of the Chagall House. Teriade publishes the Bible with his illustrations.

1958 Designs the Ravel ballet *Daphnis and Chloë* for the Paris Opera. Lectures in Chicago and Brussels. Designs stained-glass windows for Metz Cathedral.

1959 Honorary member of the American Academy of Arts and Letters. Honorary doctorate from the University of Glasgow. Exhibitions in Paris, Munich and Hamburg. Mural for the theatre in Frankfurt.

Chagall with his wife Bella and daughter Ida, at work in his Paris studio. *The Birthday* is behind him, 1927.

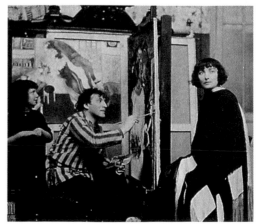

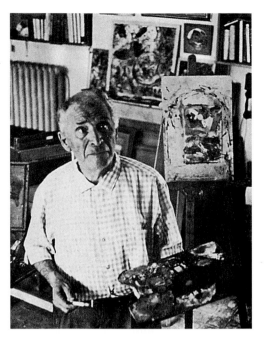

In his studio.

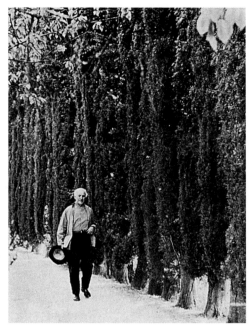

Walking in the park in Vence.

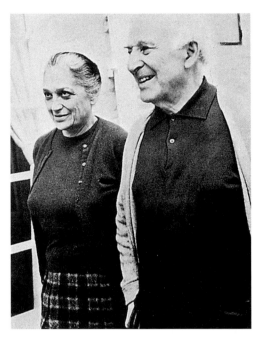

Chagall with his second wife, Vava.

1960 Together with Kokoschka he receives the Erasmus Prize in Copenhagen. Windows for the synagogue of the Hadassah University clinic in Jerusalem.

1962 Travels to Jerusalem for the consecration of the windows. Completes the Metz Cathedral windows. Is given the freedom of Vence.

1963 Retrospectives in Tokyo and Kyoto. Travels to Washington.

1964 Travels to New York. Glass windows for the United Nations building. Completes paintings for the ceiling of the Paris Opera House.

1965 Murals in Tokyo and Tel Aviv. Starts on paintings for the new Metropolitan Opera and the Lincoln Center in New York, and designs for *The Magic Flute*. Is made an Officer of the Legion of Honour.

1966 Mosaics and twelve wall panels for the new parliament building in Jerusalem. Travels to New York for the unveiling of his work for the Lincoln Center. Moves from Vence to his newly built house at nearby Saint-Paul-de-Vence. Completes *Exodus* (p. 83) and *War* (p. 84).

1967 Attends the production of Mozart's *Magic Flute* on the opening night in New York. Retrospectives to mark his 80th birthday in Zurich and Cologne. Designs three large-scale tapestries for the parliament building in Jerusalem.

1968 Travels to Washington. Glass windows for Metz Cathedral. Mosaic for the University of Nice.

1969 Lays the foundation stone of the Message Biblique Institute in Nice. Travels to Israel for the unveiling of his tapestries in the parliament building.

1970 His stained-glass windows for the Zurich Minster are consecrated. *Homage to Chagall* exhibition in the Grand Palais, Paris.

1972 Begins work on a mosaic for the First National Bank, Chicago.

1973 Travels to Moscow and Leningrad. The Musée national Message Biblique Marc Chagall is opened in Nice.

1974 His windows for Reims Cathedral are consecrated. He travels to Russia, and to Chicago for the unveiling of his mosaic.

In a café in Saint-Paul-de-Vence.

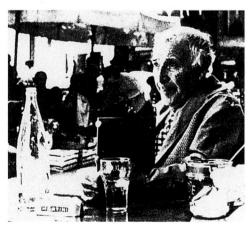

1975–6 Exhibition of works done on paper in Chicago. Travelling show in five Japanese cities. *The Fall of Icarus* (p. 88).

1977–8 The French president confers on Chagall the Grand Cross of the Legion of Honour. Visits Italy and Israel. Starts work on windows for St Stephen's in Mainz. Exhibition in Florence.

1979–80 Exhibitions in New York and Geneva. *The Psalms of David* in Musée national Message Biblique in Nice.

1981–2 Exhibition of his graphic works in Hanover, Paris and Zurich. Retrospective in the Moderna Museet in Stockholm and the Louisiana Museum in Humlebrek, Denmark (until March 1983).

1984 Retrospectives in the Centre Pompidou in Paris, and in Nice, Saint-Paul-de-Vence, Rome and Basle.

1985 Retrospective at the Royal Academy of Art in London and at the Philadelphia Museum of Art. On 28 March, Chagall dies at Saint-Paul-de-Vence. Retrospective shows of his works done on paper in Hanover, Chicago and Zurich.

Photo Credits

The publishers would like to express their thanks to the archives, museums, private collections, galleries and photographers for their kind support in the production of this book and for making their pictures available. If not stated otherwise, the reproductions were made from material from the archive of the publishers. In addition to the institutions and collections named in the picture descriptions, special mention is made of the following:

© akg-images: pp. 31, 41, 55, 72, 78
© akg-images/Erich Lessing: p. 39
© ARTOTHEK: pp. 32, 85

© Joachim Blauel/ARTOTHEK: pp. 47, 73, 81
© The Bridgeman Art Library: pp. 10 top, 14, 18, 53, 60, 66/67, 74, 79, 83
© Christie's Images/ARTOTHEK: pp. 76, 90
© Photo CNAC/MNAM, Dist. RMN – Droits réservés: pp. 45, 88
© Photo CNAC/MNAM, Dist. RMN – Philippe Migeat: p. 43
© Photo CNAC/MNAM, Dist. RMN – Adam Rzepka: p. 59
David Heald © The Solomon R. Guggenheim Foundation, New York: pp. 27, 49
© Hans Hinz/ARTOTHEK: pp. 30, 33
© 2011 Kunsthaus Zürich. All rights reserved: pp. 11, 84

© Kunstsammlung Nordrhein-Westfalen, Düsseldorf/Photo: Walter Klein: p. 2
Philippe Migeat, Paris © Musée national d'art moderne, Centre Georges Pompidou, Paris: pp. 25, 61
© The Museum of Modern Art, New York: pp. 21, 38
© Philadelphia Museum of Art, Philadelphia: pp. 17, 34, 37, 52
© SCALA, Florence: p. 89
© Stedelijk Museum, Amsterdam: p. 75
© 2011 Tate, London: p. 40
© Peter Willi/ARTOTHEK: p. 69